Praise for *Say Goodbye to Survival Mode*

Imagine stopping the frantic pace of our hurried lives to regain peace and purpose. Crystal's book, full of practical insights and helpful advice, will help us do just that. This invaluable resource is like having a personal time and money manager at your fingertips.

—Lysa TerKeurst, *New York Times* best-selling author and president of Proverbs 31

We've exhausted ourselves by overcommitting and trying to maintain such crazy schedules that we can't even find a time slot to take a breath from it all. This book will give you that breath of air. For the woman who does it *all*, take a few minutes to read Crystal Paine's new book, *Say Goodbye to Survival Mode*. You won't regret it!

—Claire Diaz-Ortiz, author, speaker, and innovator at Twitter, Inc.

Crystal Paine candidly shares her journey of how she learned to live a life of purpose and intention in *Say Goodbye to Survival Mode*. This book is a perfect blend of how-to, no-nonsense advice and friendly coffee talk with a trusted friend.

—Stephanie O'Dea is a *New York Times* best-selling author, slow cooking expert, and blogger at StephanieODea.com

The weight of the world began rolling off my shoulders somewhere between the first and second chapter. The advice is not earth-shattering but it is life-altering. It is the simplicity of what Crystal shares, and the openness by which she does it, that allows for us to *Say Goodbye to Survival Mode* and hello to our best life yet.

—Fawn Weaver, author of *Happy Wives Club* and founder of HappyWivesClub.com Ministries

Crystal Paine is the down-to-earth, genuine mom you need to learn from—have your highlighter ready! This book is packed with experiential wisdom, practical helps, and "you-can-do-this" encouragements that will give you hope and catapult you into action!

—Tracey Eyster, author of *Be the Mom* and founder of FamilyLife's MomLife Today

Wow, every busy woman needs to read this book! Crystal very clearly identifies the habits that lead to the "barely surviving" feelings so many of us have, which eventually lead to burnout. And she offers very practical and insightful solutions. I have long admired Crystal's ability to create and stick with good boundaries and habits, which is a big reason for her success! I'm so grateful she's sharing her secrets!

—Shaunti Feldhahn, social researcher and
best-selling author of *For Women Only*

I love, love, love this book. Crystal challenges me at each priority to be intentional, purposeful, and to plan strategically so that I can cultivate a more centered life. *Say Goodbye to Survival Mode* has so many practical suggestions, great stories relevant to my life, and inspiration to live life well.

—Sally Clarkson, author of *Desperate,
Mission of Motherhood,* and other books
and blogger at ITakeJoy.com

The scheduling monster can easily take every spare minute you have available and is something I battle regularly. Crystal walks us through how to tame the beast and prioritize what's important, leaving us with time to both recharge and pursue our passions.

—Barbara Rainey, cofounder of FamilyLife

In her warm, been-there-done-that tone, Crystal guides you past mere survival and gives you practical steps you need to live the kind of life you were designed to live, with renewed encouragement and a whole lotta hope.

—Kathi Lipp, speaker and author of *The Husband
Project* and *The Get Yourself Organized Project*

What I love about Crystal is her rare ability to combine thought-provoking, tangible advice and practical tips with a heartfelt passion for better living. She brings the reader into her not-so-perfect (thank goodness) world, where she reminds us of all the ways she has put her own words into practice many times. The bottom line is that there is a life worth living, no matter where you are, and Crystal is going to speak right to your heart in *Say Goodbye to Survival Mode.*

—Angie Smith, best-selling author of *What
Women Fear, I Will Carry You,* and *Mended*

Say

GOODBYE

to

SURVIVAL
MODE

9 SIMPLE STRATEGIES TO **STRESS LESS,**
SLEEP MORE, AND **RESTORE YOUR PASSION** FOR LIFE

CRYSTAL PAINE

NELSON
BOOKS

An Imprint of Thomas Nelson

Published in Nashville, Tennessee, by Nelson Books, an imprint of Thomas Nelson. Nelson Books and Thomas Nelson are registered trademarks of HarperCollins Christian Publishing, Inc.

Published in association with The Fedd Agency, thefeddagency.com.

Thomas Nelson, Inc., titles may be purchased in bulk for educational, business, fund-raising, or sales promotional use. For information, please e-mail SpecialMarkets@ ThomasNelson.com.

In some instances, names, dates, locations, and other identifying details have been changed to protect the identities and privacy of those mentioned in this book.

This publication is intended to provide authoritative information in regard to the subject matter covered. The publisher and author are not engaged in rendering medical or other professional services and do not have financial or commercial interest in any of the products, services, or professionals mentioned in this book. If you require medical advice or other expert assistance, you should seek the services of a competent professional.

The websites recommended in this book are intended as resources for the reader. These websites are not intended in any way to be or to imply an endorsement on behalf of Thomas Nelson, nor does the publisher vouch for their content for the life of this book.

Scripture quotations are taken from the THE ENGLISH STANDARD VERSION. © 2001 by Crossway Bibles, a division of Good News Publishers.

Library of Congress Cataloging-in-Publication Data

Paine, Crystal.
 Say goodbye to survival mode : 9 simple strategies to stress less, sleep more, and restore your passion for life / Crystal Paine.
   pages cm
 Includes bibliographical references.
 ISBN 978-1-4002-0646-9
 1. Women—Conduct of life. 2. Stress management for women. 3. Time management.
 I. Title.
 BJ1610.P256 2014
 248.8'43—dc23   2013027588

Printed in the United States of America

14 15 16 17 18 RRD 6 5 4 3 2

To my children: Kathrynne, Kaitlynn, and Silas

When I was in the pit of postpartum depression, it was love for you that kept me going. You've turned my world upside down, kept me on my knees, and taught me a depth of love I didn't know existed. Thank you for being excited about Mommy writing another book—and also for constantly reminding me that real life matters much more than the words I type on the computer.

I love you to the moon and back!

Contents ■■■■■■■■■■■■■■■■■■■■■■■

Introduction ▮▮▮▮▮▮▮▮▮▮▮▮▮▮▮▮▮

Frazzled, Tired, and Behind?
You're Not Alone

Ask a friend, an acquaintance, or even a stranger how she's doing, and more than likely, she'll sigh and say some variation of, "I'm so busy. I can barely breathe most days just trying to survive. You know how that goes" (insert forced smile).

Sadly, yes. Most of us do know the feeling. We are busy juggling a way-too-long to-do list, and we can't seem to get ahead—or even just get the basics crossed off many days. We wake up every morning feeling frazzled, tired, and behind. We can't imagine living any other way—though we want to.

I can relate because I've been there. A few years ago, I was stressed and exhausted. I had three young children, a husband who had a brand-new business, and a thriving blog of my own that required at least forty hours of work per week to keep afloat. This was more than enough to fill my waking hours each day, but instead of realizing this, I unwisely said yes to numerous other good things until I landed myself into near-breakdown state. It was only then that I woke up to how out of control my life and schedule were.

After months of relearning habits, reworking priorities, and retraining thought patterns, I've become a new woman: one who is energized, excited about life, passionate, purposeful, healthy, and rested. This book shares my story of saying good-bye to survival mode. It's raw, vulnerable, and candid—and not a story I ever thought I'd write a book about. But after years of blogging, writing, and speaking to women, I knew that I wasn't alone in my struggles.

When I started my blog, MoneySavingMom.com, my desire was to give women practical, hands-on information on ways they could save money. I quickly discovered that many people desperately wanted to change their financial outlooks, but they didn't have an ounce of time or energy left to devote to their finances with everything else they had on their plates. The majority of women had so much going on in their lives that they felt they were just barely surviving. Take, for instance, this note I received from Darcy:

> I'm a brand-new mom of a newborn, and I have my own business. I'm so happy that I found your blog, but I feel like I discovered it at a time in my life when I don't have a free minute to devote to implementing what you recommend. In addition, I'm a notorious procrastinator and money waster. I sincerely want to change, but being so new to this lifestyle, so set in my bad habits, and so busy, I have no idea how to go about it.

Darcy wasn't alone in her feelings; I was getting e-mails like this from women in all walks of life—single and married moms, work-outside-the-home moms, and stay-at-home moms. All of them were saying the same thing: "We're tired. We lack purpose. We want to change our lives, but we have too much to do and not enough time. Help!"

These women wanted to escape the hamster wheel of life that had them spinning to meet other people's demands and expectations. But they didn't know how to walk away, how to say no, or how to find breathing room in their lives.

While I was trying to help people with their money and budget problems, I realized I couldn't address their financial struggles until I first helped these women deal with deeper issues, such as a lack of purpose, a loss of perspective, and a sense of hopelessness.

In 2010, after undergoing my own paradigm shift, I had a heartfelt desire to share my own experiences of how I went from simply trying to keep up with everything—my kids, business, marriage, and friends—to passionately living on purpose. The road hasn't been easy, and I've nowhere near "arrived," but the efforts and changes have definitely been worth it.

Take a few minutes, and think about your life. Do you feel burned out? Stressed to the max? Stuck?

Do you struggle with having so many things you want to do each day but lacking the motivation to get them done?

Are you having a tough time creating and adapting a routine that works for you and your family?

Do you put unrealistic expectations on yourself to have and do it all—and feel you're failing miserably?

Do you find it challenging to figure out where your priorities lie?

Again, I can relate, and I wrote this book to share the answers to these questions that I've learned and have seen others successfully answer and overcome in their own lives. This book is for you because I know there is a way out. My sincere hope is that by the end of our time together, you'll either see the light at the end of the tunnel or be out of the tunnel completely!

As you read through each chapter, soak in the life-changing principles, and take the time to do the exercises. You will learn not only why it is so important to live with intention, but I'll also teach you effective and simple strategies so you can have more purpose in your life on a daily basis.

You'll find valuable suggestions and ideas on

- how to become more self-disciplined;
- how to set and keep goals;
- how to manage your time, money, and home;
- how to juggle responsibilities and self-care;
- how to experience less stress and more joy;
- how to rediscover your passion and purpose for life; and
- how to keep a balanced life perspective and make a difference in big and small ways.

Not everything in this book will work for everyone. So please don't feel like you need to heed each suggestion or idea I share. I completely understand there is no one-size-fits-all program that will work for everyone in every stage and season of life. We each have unique personalities, viewpoints, and life circumstances, and we each need to approach things in a way that works best for ourselves and our families. So don't feel pressure to approach every aspect of your life the same way I approach mine. However, I hope that the principles in this book will inspire you to make some slow and steady changes in your life that will result in a big transformation over time.

I'm here to help you as much as I can. Use what works and save the other ideas for later, or just skip them entirely. My greatest hope for you is that you can escape from feeling stuck and find the freedom and fulfillment that comes from living your life on purpose.

You don't have to stay perpetually overwhelmed and exhausted, barely existing in survival mode, anymore. You can start living with direction and passion. Today.

1

Stop Trying to Do It All

> Happiness is not a matter of intensity but of
> balance, order, rhythm, and harmony.
>
> —THOMAS MERTON

Goal: Streamline your life and cut schedule clutter so you can focus your time and energy on the things that matter most.

Strategy: Create a personal priorities list and use it as a springboard for culling your commitments and to-do list.

I had to make the call. And I was seriously dreading it.

I was supposed to meet some friends for a fun outing that afternoon. I had been looking forward to it. What mother who barely has time for herself wouldn't be ecstatic about doing something, anything exciting? The problem was, I was already fifteen minutes late. And I wasn't even close to getting out the door.

With my feet glued to the sticky kitchen floor, I scanned the perimeter of my messy house. The dishes. The towering pile of laundry mocking me from the bedroom corner for the past week. The dust. The carpet needing to be vacuumed. The bathroom screaming for a good scrubbing. I looked at my hopelessly long to-do list I had scribbled on a scrap of paper. I watched my three, half-dressed children under the age of five all seeming to need my attention at that very moment. I swallowed hard and felt a pair of invisible hands around my neck. My palms shook with the anxiety of way too much to do.

I wanted to run away from it all. I was exhausted. I was stressed to the max. I felt stuck. I desperately fought the urge to yell, throw something, and cry—all at the same time.

Picking up the phone and admitting that I was in such an overwhelmed state (and late yet again) seemed to cement the fact that I was failing as a wife, as a mom, and as a woman.

Sure, I loved God, my husband, Jesse, and my kids (Kathrynne, age four; Kaitlynn, age two; and Silas, a baby at the time). And yes, there were still times when I felt happy and fulfilled. But more and more, those stretches were a thing of the past—experiences and feelings that seemed unfamiliar and scarce.

I wasn't living. I was merely surviving. Scared of what might happen if I couldn't find a way out of this maze of misery, I prayed I'd find help. And soon.

THE SLOW AND STEADY DOWNWARD SPIRAL

How had things come to this? How could I not even manage to get out the door to meet friends for a fun afternoon without falling apart and feeling like a colossal wreck?

In retrospect, this wasn't something that happened overnight. Instead, it was a slow progression in an unhealthy direction. It started with a lot of major changes and crises in a short amount of time.

I had been married for six years—years that had been filled with a whirlwind of life events, some of which were very stressful: pinching pennies out of necessity while my husband finished college and went to law school, having three children in less than five years, starting four different home businesses (three of which flopped), moving four times. I felt life was spinning out of control.

I was working thirty to forty hours per week as a blogger and writer to try and keep our family afloat financially. My blog, MoneySavingMom.com, which I had started in 2007, was experiencing incredible growth. It was a great thing, but by the time my third child was born in 2009, I was in over my head. Around thirty to fifty thousand people were reading my blog every day, and I was a one-woman show, running the business without any help. I was getting up too early and staying up too late almost every day and night trying to meet all my business and writing deadlines. And I was still recovering from postpartum depression.

The lies started swooping in with a vengeance. "I'm going to be okay," I whispered to myself when I felt suffocated by responsibilities and to-dos. I told everyone who asked that I was "great" and "wonderful."

But deep down, I knew the truth. I was anything but fine. A chipper attitude and wide grin couldn't mask how overwhelmed I felt.

Running at full steam started taking a toll on me physically.

Exhaustion-induced health issues began to surface. Every two to three weeks, I would be bedridden for a few days with a high fever, headache, and intense pain throughout my whole body.

As this sickness continued to hit every few weeks for four months, I became concerned. I knew what I was experiencing was not normal, and I wondered what was wrong with me. But I kept pushing myself, unwilling to admit I was the cause of my health issues.

FACADES AND GLIMPSES OF FREEDOM

In the midst of so much change and upheaval, my type-A personality me wanted to keep up the persona of perfection. I didn't stop the insanity. I didn't sit down and analyze what I could realistically handle. I didn't recognize my limits and set boundaries. Instead, I wore a plastic smile and continued to say yes.

- "Sure, I'll take on that project."
- "Sure, I'll meet that deadline."
- "Sure, I'll bake those brownies."
- "Sure, I'll look over your e-book and give you feedback."
- "Sure, I'll meet you for lunch and help you figure out how to start a blog."

As time marched on and my rope grew thinner, I kept piling on more projects and responsibilities, ignoring all the warning signs.

But that cold spring day when I had to make the phone call

telling my friends I was running behind and going to be dreadfully late, something snapped inside me. For the first time, I realized how badly my life was spiraling out of control—and that something needed to give. For my children. For my husband. And for my sanity.

I didn't make any outward changes yet, but my mind-set started changing. I stopped believing the lies that I could do it all, be it all, and have it all. I just wanted to be free again—free from the rat race, free from the burden of feeling that I had to say yes to everything, free from the pressure of trying to be perfect. I wanted to be free to enjoy life.

Though I had a long way to go to find total freedom, I had taken the first step.

THE WORDS THAT SPARKED THE ULTIMATE CHANGE

A few weeks later, after months of scrimping and saving, Jesse and I had enough to put an offer on a house we'd fallen in love with. Our offer was accepted, and a moving date was set for five weeks later.

I reveled in the joy for about a second, when the reality of the situation finally hit. *What am I thinking? I can't add the responsibilities of moving to my plate!* I was barely keeping my head above water as it was. There was no way I could find time to pack up the house in five weeks too.

I was also in the midst of helping launch an intensive training event for bloggers. Guess when this event was scheduled? Right during the time when my family was supposed to be moving!

My colleagues and I had spent months planning this blogging event, advertising it, finalizing details, securing speakers, and getting sponsors. We were excited about it and thrilled that we'd sold all the tickets in record time. The only problem was that we still had a lot more work ahead of us.

As I contemplated how on earth I was going to pull off the event and moving, all while juggling everything else going on in my life, I started to panic. In the past, when big projects were piled on my plate, I'd simply pushed harder, gotten less sleep, and powered through. This time I knew I didn't have enough steam in my engine to do that. Just considering it was completely overwhelming me.

Finally, I sat down with my husband and tearfully told him, "I can't do this anymore. I'm overwhelmed. I'm exhausted. Help!"

I was expecting a big hug or words of sympathy. And if I'm totally honest, I wanted a pat on the back for a job well done, you know, for my Superwoman efforts. I didn't receive the response I'd hoped for, but I got something better. Unfortunately, I didn't appreciate it at the time.

My husband looked at me sympathetically and then uttered some of the wisest words he's ever said to me. "Crystal, you know that you are the one who is bringing most of this on yourself."

Despite the truth and wisdom in his words, they were the last ones I wanted to hear. His statement only made me more frustrated at how stuck I felt. Instead of taking the epiphany to heart, however, I wallowed in a woe-is-me rant in my head. I felt sorry for myself and continued to blame everyone except the cause of my problems—me.

ME—THE PROBLEM AND THE SOLUTION

I mulled over what my husband said later that evening. As much as I didn't want to admit it, I knew he was right. I didn't have to spend so many hours blogging. I didn't have to be on the event-planning team for the blogger event. I didn't have to say yes to every commitment and opportunity that came my way. Nobody and nothing was obligating me to do anything except me!

Finally, I had reached my tipping point. Relief washed over me, and I felt the weight of all the burdens I was shifting around release. I had more control over my life than I realized. I could stop the madness. I could eliminate the chaos. I could start setting boundaries. I could start saying no.

Yes, I was the problem. But I was also the solution.

CHA-CHA-CHA-CHANGES

In the days that followed, I made some drastic changes. I stepped down from the event-planning project. I said no to all business offers that came my way. I shut down almost all my social media channels. I stopped feeling obligated to other people. I started making sleep a priority. I hired more help with my business. I stopped trying to be Superwoman.

Sure, some people were disappointed in me—and weren't shy to voice their opinions—but I had never felt so at peace. I finally felt like I was living. Really living.

Within a month, my health had improved dramatically. In fact, the twice-a-month, high-fever sickness disappeared within six weeks and never came back again. Even in the craziness of moving, I felt calm, not frazzled or frantic.

> They always say time changes things, but you actually have to change them yourself.
> —ANDY WARHOL

You know what surprised me the most about my new stance? My relationship with my husband did a 180-degree turnaround. Truth be told, I had been so busy spinning my wheels that I hadn't realized how bad things had gotten in my marriage. No, we weren't fighting all the time, and no one was threatening to leave. However, as with many marriages where busyness takes center stage, our communication had diminished to a purely superficial level. *How was your day, honey? Kathrynne drew a pretty picture today. That was a delicious dinner. Don't forget to pick up milk on your way home.* You know, that sort of thing.

My marriage had completely lost its spark. My daily schedule was so packed that I was missing out on some of the most important things in life. Gone were the hours my husband and I had spent laughing and enjoying each other. Gone were the deep discussions about our dreams, goals, and desires. Gone were the simple but romantic times holding hands. Those precious moments had been replaced by work, deadlines, and conference calls. There was always business stuff to do, and in the process, my marriage and my family took a backseat.

My husband had been feeling neglected for months. He felt

I was too busy for him. The only reason he didn't mention anything was because, well, I was too busy to listen.

Sadly, he was right.

During the previous two years of building my business, I'd forgotten how to breathe. I'd become a workaholic, and everyone except me seemed to know it was doing more harm than good.

AN IMPERFECT PROCESS

In the process of letting go, I admit, I've passed up a lot of great opportunities. But I'm okay with that. I've found God always provides the right projects at the right time that I can realistically manage and enjoy doing them.

Yes, there are moments when I want to dig out my Superwoman cape to impress others and hear them say how wonderful and accomplished I am. But when I remember how empty and exhausted it felt to try to do it all, I realize it's okay never to wear the cape again.

Now let me be clear: my life isn't perfect. There are times when I've gotten off-course and have temporarily taken too much upon myself. But when that happens, I have a trusted group of friends who help me get back on track. I've asked these people to keep me accountable for having margin and breathing room in my life and to call me out when they see me sliding down the slippery slope of heaping my plate too full. I also remind myself regularly how bad things were a few years ago, and that helps me to be quick to make changes lest things get out of hand again.

I'd rather do a few things well, have my priorities in order, and enjoy life than try to do two hundred things poorly and have a stressed-out, exhausted, passionless existence.

JUST SAY NO

Time doesn't expand limitlessly. When I say yes to one thing, I must say no to something else. For example, if I choose to make getting up early a priority, I have to say no to staying up late on a regular basis. It also means I have to routinely say no to worthwhile activities and events that would keep me out late. In order to say yes, I must learn to say no.

> You have to decide what your highest priorities are and have the courage—pleasantly, smilingly, nonapologetically, to say "no" to other things. And the way you do that is by having a bigger "yes" burning inside. The enemy of the "best" is often the "good."
> —STEPHEN COVEY

I don't like saying no. But if my struggles and health issues a few years ago taught me anything, it was this: If I want to live a productive, efficient, happy, peaceful, and disciplined life, I must learn to say no. And I must say it often.

If you want to stick with and accomplish your goals, you're going to have to get good at saying no. It's hard to do, especially if you're an overachiever like me. This is a foreign concept, I know. We are taught that we need to be "yes women." We worry what people will think of us if we don't attend everything we're invited to, respond to every call for volunteers, or be on every committee.

But how can we stress less, sleep more, and restore our passion for life while trying to balance a full set of spinning plates? We can't. Living with intention means saying no to the things that aren't important to us so we can say yes to what matters most. If you're used to saying yes to everything and everyone, making the change to choosing well is going to be a challenge in the beginning. But once you start doing it, the benefits you'll reap will be so worth it that I promise you'll begin to do it even more!

WHAT YOU WANT TO KNOW

Q: I'm a stay-at-home mom to a five-week-old baby boy. I have been following your blog for several years, and I've always admired how much you accomplish in a day. Before my son was born, I had a full-time job and used that as my excuse not to do everything, but now that I'm a stay-at-home mom, I still can't seem to do everything. Do you ever have a day that you just relax and not worry about getting everything done?

A: There are days when I fantasize about a to-do list that has everything crossed off, and then I quickly realize that this is just not going to happen. So I have two choices: I can do the best I can with the time and energy I have, or I can spend my life frustrated at everything left undone.

Mothering is a 24/7 gig, so I've learned that there's

no such thing as a complete "day off." That said, I know my limits and try to take a few hours of respite and refreshment at least once a week. This might be sitting and reading a good book, snuggling for an hour with my children, watching a movie with my husband, going to a coffee shop, shopping by myself, doing something with a friend, or taking a bubble bath or afternoon nap.

We also try to take Sundays completely off at our house. I don't blog or answer e-mails and often don't even turn on my computer or phone! We typically spend the day at church, hanging out with friends and family, talking, reading, and yes, sleeping. I look forward to this one unplugged day every week. It refreshes, reenergizes, and renews me for the week ahead.

THE FOUR Cs TO CREATING MARGIN

Does any part of my story resonate with you? Can you relate to my breakdown? Or my unhealthy need to say yes to too many things? Do you feel like you're drowning? Merely surviving in life instead of thriving?

There are things you can do, starting today, that will help bring sanity, joy, and purpose back into your life. When you are stretched, frazzled, overwhelmed, and spent from following packed schedules, tackling never-ending to-do lists, and being pulled in every direction, you need margin. You need to eliminate certain things from your life that will give you breathing room.

I like how Dr. Richard Swenson describes margin in his book *Margin: Restoring Emotional, Physical, Financial, and Time Reserves to Overloaded Lives.* He writes, "Margin is the gap between rest and exhaustion, the space between breathing freely and suffocating."[1]

Here are four ways to find that space. If you have an hour or so, treat each section below like an exercise to point you toward the margin you so desperately need. Plus, getting clarity now will be helpful as we move forward in this book. We'll keep hitting these themes.

Create a Personal Priorities List

Take thirty minutes, and sit down somewhere quiet. Use this time to craft a list of four to six personal priorities in the space provided or in your personal journal. You will use this list as a foundation to determine your schedule, responsibilities, and to-dos in the next chapter.

Ask yourself the following questions to figure out what you want to see on this list. What is most important to you? Family? Work? Health? Others? Where do you see yourself in twenty-five years? At the end of your life, what do you want to look back on and have accomplished? What's going to matter most to you?

Start writing down your ideas. As you do, you'll likely see patterns developing. Take note of these patterns to help you determine what really matters to you.

Remember, this is *your* personal priorities list, not someone else's list. Catch yourself every time you start to write things down based upon the opinions of others (e.g., "I should probably include being involved in the PTA because that's what the other moms would do.").

MY PERSONAL PRIORITIES LIST

....

....

....

....

....

Once you have some ideas jotted down, divide them where applicable into the following categories:

- Personal (personal growth, physical health)
- Spiritual and Emotional (relationship with God, involvement in church)
- Family (relationship with your husband, children, and extended family)
- Career/Ministry (finances, business projects, volunteer opportunities)
- Friendships

You don't have to include all these categories, or you can include others I may not have mentioned. I'm giving you these examples to guide you. Create categories based on your unique situation, whether you are married or not, have children or not, have a career or are a stay-at-home mom. I highly recommend, however, including at least two of these categories as priorities to give you a healthy balance in life. For instance, exercising is important, and something I highly recommend. But if you set a goal to exercise for six hours every day and don't plan to spend any time on your finances or building relationships, you're probably going to run into some serious issues in the not-too-distant future.

Also keep in mind that we all have unique family situations, needs, commitments, strengths, and weaknesses. What works for one person won't necessarily work for another. And what works in one season of our lives might not work at all in another season.

We're going to flesh out these categories and ideas in the next chapter, but this exercise gives you a solid backdrop to prioritize what you should focus on and do on a daily basis. If choosing four to six things seems hard for you, challenge yourself to do it anyway. The very process of listing things will help you figure out where your priorities lie. And remember that you can change this list at any time. What you write down now doesn't have to be set in stone for the rest of your life!

If you're curious, here are my personal priorities right now:

- Have a strong and vibrant relationship with the Lord.
- Maintain a wonderful relationship with my husband.
- Spend quality and quantity time with my children.
- Nurture my body and soul through rest, nutrition, margin, exercise, and reading, and constantly challenge myself to learn and grow as a person.
- Write, speak, and manage my blog and business.

Clear the Schedule Clutter

I'm well known by my friends and family as a minimalist. I disdain clutter and owning stuff that I don't love, use, or need.

I admit I can get a little OCD about it to the point that I get rid of stuff that I really should keep.

For instance, I have two pairs of jeans that I wear in the fall and winter with boots. I don't know what I was thinking, but in one of my ruthless clean-the-house-from-top-to-bottom rampages last year, I put both pairs of those jeans in the garage sale box. I wasn't wearing them (since, hello, it was summer!), so I figured I could get rid of them.

A few months later, when the weather turned colder, I realized that I didn't have any jeans to wear with my boots. *How weird*, I thought. I was sure I had some jeans around from last winter. Lo and behold, as I prepared for an upcoming garage sale, guess what I found in one of my "for sale" boxes? That's right. My two pairs of jeans. I had a good laugh at myself and my obsessive clutter-ridding nature.

Though I have a tendency to go overboard in eliminating clutter, I'd rather have to occasionally replace something that I inadvertently got rid of than have a house cluttered with stuff I don't need or use. I've learned that either we control the clutter or the clutter will control us. If we don't keep on top of the stuff that seems to breed in our closets when we're sleeping at night, it will soon overtake our houses and our lives.

It's the same way with our schedules. Many times busyness is mistakenly equated with productivity. But those two words are not synonymous. Just because we are spinning our wheels, rushing from one commitment to the next, doesn't necessarily mean that we are doing anything worthwhile.

If we don't carefully guard our days and regularly weed out the unnecessary from our schedules, pretty soon our schedules will be packed to the max with unwanted to-dos we got dragged into out of obligation or because we didn't give ourselves the option to say no. If we want to say goodbye to survival mode, we need to make time for what really matters. This means we have to clear out the nonessential commitments.

As we've already established, we've got to learn to say no. This is the first step in finding margin and fulfillment in life. But we don't want to say no to everything, so how do we figure out what is worth doing?

Creating a personal priorities list is vital in enabling us to determine what is truly important and what opportunities we can pass up. After all, if we don't know what is most important to us, how we will know it when it comes our way?

I recently read the book *Leading on Empty* by Wayne Cordeiro. The author suggests writing a list of activities and commitments that currently seem to run your life and then determining whether they rejuvenate and energize you or drain and exhaust you. I found it helpful to consider all my activities in this light. Take some time out of your day, and try this!

If you felt inadequate in any way when you read my personal priorities list, let me set your mind at ease. I might have a few things that I do well, but there are many things I don't do at all.

Yes, I homeschool my children, run a widely read blog, and keep my grocery budget low, but that's because I stick to simple meals, don't have a garden, don't sew, don't even attempt to decorate my house, send my husband's dress clothes to the dry cleaner instead of ironing them, don't watch TV except for the occasional show online, rarely go shopping for anything other than groceries, and only have my children involved in a few extracurricular activities.

But wait! There's more: I also don't take care of any of the bill paying or bookkeeping; my husband does this as he's excellent at it and loves it. We don't have pets to care for. I'm not in any regular playgroups or Bible study groups. I'm not on any committees. I don't pack lunches for my husband to take to work. And I only make dinner four to five nights per week. (We eat out one night a week and eat dinner with extended family one to two nights each week.)

If skipping similar to-dos sounds like a blissful utopia to you, then you probably have some clutter in your schedule. Time to treat your calendar to a rigorous makeover!

You see, when you spend the bulk of your days doing things that really matter—things that make a difference, which help you move closer to your overall goals that are really going to matter to you in twenty-five years—you can't help but feel like you're actually doing something and going somewhere with your life.

Cut Out Time and Energy Suckers

Last year I deleted my personal Facebook account. Well, I didn't exactly delete it. I still have it up so I can run the Money Saving Mom® Facebook page, but I unfriended everyone on my personal Facebook profile. Harsh? Maybe, but I didn't unfriend everyone because I was fed up with Facebook or because someone on the site had offended me.

I deleted it because, for me, Facebook had become a time and energy sucker. A five-minute Facebook break in the middle of a writing or blogging project would turn into twenty-five minutes or more. I'd get sucked in to this virtual world of viewing other people's pictures, commenting on their statuses, reading through conversations (sometimes I didn't even know any of the people—pathetic, I know!), and responding to the many messages that came through my Facebook inbox.

Facebook had become a time-wasting distraction for me, so I finally got rid of it. You know what's amazing? Once I stopped using my personal account, I couldn't figure out how I had time to log on in the first place! Sure, I'm not always up on the latest news on everyone, but I certainly stay a lot more focused during my online time.

Best of all, I've found that people go out of their way to call, e-mail, text, or tell me things in person since they know I won't see it on their Facebook pages. I feel like my face-to-face relationships with friends have grown stronger now that I'm not tied down to social networking.

Maybe Facebook isn't an area in which you struggle. But can you think of other time and energy suckers that you could amputate from your life? Like TV? Movies? Internet browsing? Blog hopping? Pinterest? Texting? Relationships? Shopping?

An eye-opening way to figure out what's eating up your daily allotment of hours is to keep a time log of everything you do every thirty minutes for at least two or three days. While this exercise might seem tedious, I'm willing to bet you'll realize you truly do have more time than you think. You might also be surprised to see how much time you waste on things that are meaningless.

Count the Costs

There's an important question I ask myself before I commit to anything: What are the consequences if I say yes to this?

For example, will saying yes to a late-night activity mean that I won't be able to get up early in the morning? Will saying yes to a big commitment mean that my home and family will suffer?

Count the cost of each commitment before you make your decision. Don't blindly say yes when someone tries to convince you that you must do something. Don't give in to peer pressure or make decisions based on what people might think of you if you say no.

Recently, I was invited to go to a conference that I really, really wanted to attend. The conference coordinators offered to pay all my travel expenses, put me up in a nice hotel, and proposed coordinating a get-together with some women I've wanted to meet for a long time. There were no strings attached; they just wanted me to show up and have a wonderful time.

I was giddy as I thought about this conference and what an amazing opportunity it was. I excitedly showed my husband the e-mail, fully expecting he'd want me to jump on the opportunity. He surprised me by saying, "That sounds neat, but you know you can't go. We already made a commitment to go on vacation as a family that week." Oh yeah, that vacation had totally slipped my mind in the midst of my enthusiasm.

"Couldn't we postpone or change the vacation?" I pleaded. "I've been hoping to have a chance to network with these women for a long time. It would be crazy to turn down this offer."

He looked at me and said, "It's a great opportunity, and I'm glad they reached out to you, but you know that your family is more important. We've all been looking forward to this trip. I don't have any other weeks I can get off work for quite a while, and the kids will be so disappointed if we don't go."

I knew he was right. As much as this looked like an offer I'd be a fool to refuse, my commitment to my family took precedence. Besides, since this company reached out to me in the first place, there's a good chance they might be open to another similar opportunity down the road. I turned down the offer, and I don't regret it one bit. My kids are only young once; there will always be another business opportunity.

Now, that said, I don't turn down all invitations to conferences. In fact, I usually travel at least two weekends a month for business, whether it's for a media appearance, a speaking engagement, or a conference. But I evaluate each of these opportunities with my husband in light of our family priorities, my personal priorities, and what our family has already committed to during the same time period. If in doubt, I always say no. I'd rather err on the side of caution and margin than overextend myself to the detriment of my health and family.

Don't be afraid to say no. Women love to please others, and sometimes we do so at our own expense. Focus on your list of priorities. If saying no to something means your attention is drawn to what matters most—trust me, it's a good thing.

> Caving in to demands that are emotionally overwhelming, relationally unhealthy, physically exhausting, and spiritually inauthentic is not the way to create the space and rest we all need. This dilemma is best solved by understanding and establishing boundaries.
> —RICHARD SWENSON

▪▪▪▪▪▪▪▪▪▪ GET PRACTICAL ▪▪▪▪▪▪▪▪▪▪

Practice saying no. Get in the habit of saying no more often than you say yes. Over the next week, make a concerted effort not to say yes to anything right off the bat. In addition, when you make your to-do list for tomorrow, force yourself to immediately eliminate three things from your list. This is not a mind trick to make you feel more productive than you really are. Instead, it's a way to help you start learning to give yourself some breathing room and to start evaluating your to-do list in light of what has to be done and what can wait, if need be.

Pruning away the excess commitments can seem daunting at first. But I promise if you put forth the effort to stop trying to do it all, it will free you to be able to focus your energy on those things that really matter. And this will bring you so much more fulfillment and joy in life than that heaping to-do list ever will!

2

Say Yes to the Best

Time is what we want most, but what we use worst.
—WILLIAM PENN

> **Goal:** Determine your most important priorities in life, and build your schedule around those priorities.
>
> **Strategy:** Develop a best stuff list, based on your personal priorities list from chapter 1. Create a daily routine based on this best stuff list.

Whenever I go grocery shopping, I try to carry every bag from the car to the house in one trip. I've always been this way.

Back when my husband and I lived in a basement apartment and our first child, Kathrynne, was just a baby, I would always play macho-woman when it came to wrangling grocery bags. I'd make the long trek from the parking lot to the apartment with one hand holding Kathrynne's car seat carrier and every available centimeter of finger space on the other hand gripping the enormous load of shopping loot. My fingers and arm would cry out in pain under the load. I usually barely made it in the front door without dropping at least one bag. But I didn't care. I was determined to get the whole load into the house in one trip.

START WITH THE BEST STUFF FIRST

Apparently I'm not the only one who does this, as I recently found a cartoon on Pinterest with a stick figure trying to finagle about fifteen grocery bags. The caption underneath read, "Two trips are for pansies." I posted this cartoon on my Money Saving Mom® Facebook page, and thousands of women agreed they have the same mentality.

This grocery-bag juggling act reminds me how often we try to load up our schedules with an unbearable weight of things, even ones that are good.

We try so hard to do everything at once. In addition to caring for our children and our jobs, we say yes to the bake sale, yes to the PTA meeting, yes to lunch with our neighbors, yes to another work project, yes to hosting dinner for three families from church, yes to planning that party, and yes to leading that small group. Often we feel like if we say no or drop the ball, the ship's going to go down. But in reality, the only thing that's going down is our own sanity!

Here's the deal. Just like it's crazy to try to carry thirteen bags of groceries into the house in one trip, it's equally ridiculous to try to say yes to everything. We can choose to make two or three trips to bring in all the groceries. It might take a little more time, but at least you won't drop any bags or snap your back out of place. That double-bagged gallon of milk won't go sour if you leave it in the trunk for a couple more minutes. (But be sure to get the ice cream!)

PICK AND CHOOSE THE BEST STUFF

Living with purpose means wisely choosing and committing to a few of the best things for the season of life you're in. These top priorities will comprise what we're going to call your best stuff list—the list of things you will intentionally wrap your life, time, and energy around right now.

How do you figure out what should be on your best stuff list? To get you started, refer to the personal priorities list you created in the previous chapter. Your best stuff list will be directly connected to what you wrote down.

Take your personal priorities list, and flesh it out to determine your full-fledged best stuff list. Not only will this exercise give you clearer direction for where you should be focusing your time and effort, but it will also enable you to make wiser decisions on what you need to cut from your life and schedule.

If you have two young children and another one on the way, you may need to focus more on your family than adding a three-day-per-week volunteer job. If you are focused on completing your MBA, redecorating your home likely isn't going to be at the top of your list.

Now, does this mean you can't ever do anything that's not related in some way, shape, or form to your best stuff list? Of course not! But saying yes to the best means focusing and streamlining your time, energy, and efforts on what matters most at the time.

I'll share my best stuff list with you as an example (you'll notice that this is just my personal priorities list a little more in-depth).

- **Have a strong and vibrant relationship with the Lord.** As a Christian, my relationship with the Lord is my number one priority. God's grace is what sustains and strengthens me and gives me hope and joy. Spend thirty minutes reading the Bible and praying first thing in the morning. Read spiritually uplifting books, and regularly attend our local church.
- **Maintain a wonderful relationship with my husband.** It's the little things that keep the spark alive in a marriage. Flirt with my husband at least once a day. Take time to discuss disagreements and sort through conflict. Set aside time every day to spend as a couple. Plan at least one monthly date where we leave our children and go out to dinner or do something fun together.
- **Spend quality and quantity time with my children.** Next to God and my husband, my children are my top priority. In addition to reading, teaching, discipling, and playing with them, spend at least fifteen minutes with each child one-on-one every day. Take each child on an outing every few weeks.
- **Nurture my body and soul.** If I'm exhausted and burned out, I'm not a good wife and mom. Try to exercise at least four hours each week. Get at least seven hours of sleep every night, drink a lot of water, and eat at least one big salad every day. Improve my mind by reading and learning new things. Go somewhere alone for at least a few hours each week to get refreshed.

- **Write, speak, and manage my blog and business.** God has blessed my blog far beyond what I would have ever imagined. I want to wisely steward the platform He has given me and be faithful to using my gifts and passion to encourage, inspire, and bless others. Invest a significant portion of time each week to blogging, managing my team, preparing for upcoming events, and brainstorming new business ideas and strategies. Travel a few times each month for speaking engagements and other business opportunities.

My best stuff list might seem overwhelming to you or filled with items that aren't important to where you are in life. Don't worry about it. Our lives are different! One thing our lists should have in common, though, is their long-term values. For me, this list reflects what will matter to me in twenty-five years. Yours should too!

Write down your best stuff list in the space provided or in your personal journal. And keep it handy. You'll need to refer to it periodically throughout this book.

MY BEST STUFF LIST

....

....

....

....

....

Remind yourself that there are seasons of life. Your children are only young once. You will eventually graduate from college. You won't indefinitely train for a marathon. You have your whole life before you to take on some of the other things.

In the meantime, align your time with the best. Pace yourself. Be strategic (even ruthless) in how you manage your day. Then you'll be able to enjoy the journey of life instead of struggling under the weight of carrying all those proverbial bags of groceries.

MIX YOUR GIFTS WITH THE BEST STUFF

I first heard the concept of focusing on what you're uniquely gifted at in Laura Vanderkam's excellent book *168 Hours: You Have More Time Than You Think*. She challenges readers to find and exercise what she calls "core competencies."[1] These are things that you are really good at, areas where you excel. Like those double chocolate brownies you baked and everyone raved about, saying, "You should sell these!" Or when you helped your friend organize the details of her wedding day and found yourself in the zone as a wedding planner.

Right about now, you might be shaking your head and thinking, *But I'm not good at anything.* Of course you are! You might just need a little help recognizing your talents. If so, ask a friend or colleague to tell you what your top three strengths are. No matter your age or aptitude, you have special talents, abilities, and interests—things you love to do, things you do well, and things that make you feel alive.

You may have an entrepreneurial spirit, a knack for writing, or a gift of organization. Crunching numbers, cooking and baking, or babysitting the neighborhood kids might come easily to you. Maybe you enjoy budgeting, encouraging others, or serving those in need. Many of us have buried our gifts because we're too afraid of failure or rejection to even consider digging them out and using them.

DON'T TRY TO BE SOMEONE ELSE

I have almost zero talent when it comes to domestic creativity. Ask me a question about starting a business or marketing, and I can give you a hundred and one great ideas. But ask me to decorate your home or plan a party, and I'll stand there like a deer caught in the headlights. I might as well try to translate the Declaration of Independence into Mandarin.

For years, this made me feel inferior. I'd see women who could whip out hand-smocked dresses, cook amazing meals, decorate fancy wedding cakes, put together designer-looking outfits from thrift store finds, and do it all with ease and grace.

And then there was me.

I seemed to ruin almost every craft project I tried. I took a cake-decorating class once. I liked the challenge, but there was no way anyone would pay for (or even take for free) my lopsided creations. And designer-looking outfits? It's the last thing that comes to mind when describing my fashion style.

What I lacked in skill and finesse, I made up for in determination. I took sewing and baking classes. I read blog posts on being a budget fashionista. I tried my hardest to develop the talent and style that all these women seemed to have. But most of my efforts ended in failure and left me feeling defeated at my lack of ability. Not to mention that I was wasting a lot of time. I spent hours and even days focusing on things that had nothing to do with my best stuff and that I wasn't naturally good at doing.

When I started examining my skill sets and core competencies, I realized that the problem wasn't that I didn't have skills and gifts. The problem was that I was trying to be someone I wasn't created to be.

Instead of beating myself up over what I can't do, I'm learning to appreciate, focus on, and exercise those areas where I have natural abilities. And I have found much joy in being who God has created me to be, not in trying to be someone else. This has also helped me spend my time more efficiently, with purpose, and in areas that best benefit my family and me.

Have you spent too much time trying to be as domestic, artistic, creative, organized, or poetic as your best friend or sister instead of appreciating and focusing on your natural gifts? How does it make you feel when you can't measure up to someone else's innate abilities? What are some of your talents that you can start using instead of trying to mimic someone else's? Write down your answers, and use them to help you get and stay focused on your God-given gifts and talents.

GIVE YOUR GIFTS A CHANCE

Oftentimes we have gifts we didn't even know we had because we've always told ourselves, "I could never do *that!*" That was me when it came to public speaking. For years, the thought of speaking in front of an audience scared me to the point of nausea. I would do everything I could to avoid it.

In fact, when my husband and I were first married, I was asked to give a workshop at a conference. For some reason, I accepted the invitation. About two months before the event, the reality of saying yes kicked in. I started getting really, really nervous. I pictured myself in front of that little room of people, and I freaked out. Six weeks before the conference was scheduled, I e-mailed the coordinators to back out. Juvenile, I know, but that's how scared I was.

Fast-forward four years when I was asked to speak on a panel at a blogging conference. While the thought still made me anxious, I loved helping new bloggers. My passion motivated me to give it a shot. Also, I figured being on a panel with three other people couldn't be all that bad, right? So with a mixture of trepidation and excitement, I accepted the invitation.

Guess what? A few months before the conference, I was browsing through the event's website and noticed that I was advertised as one of the keynote speakers. I about fell out of my chair. Not only that, but I was slated to be the opening night keynote speaker. Talk about freaking out!

I'm not sure what got into me, but this time I didn't squirm my way out of the conference. I decided to embrace the speaking opportunity, though it made me feel physically ill. I read the word-for-word speech I wrote while my knees knocked, my voice quivered, and my hands shook. It was probably one of the most poorly given keynote speeches in the history of mankind, but my heart was behind every word—even if the delivery was pathetic. And when my talk was over, I realized something surprising. There was a tiny part of me that enjoyed the experience.

I've since gone on to face my fear of public speaking. Over the last four years, I've spoken in front of audiences from a few dozen to a few thousand. The funny thing is I now enjoy public speaking. In fact, I'm finding more and more that public speaking energizes me. I love communicating concepts, sharing stories from my life that resonate with others, and giving women hope in the struggles they face. Best of all, I love the opportunity to have in-depth, one-on-one conversations with the attendees afterward where we unpack their heartaches and burdens and I help them feel encouraged and excited about life.

Never in a hundred years would I have pictured myself enjoying public speaking, but I really do. Had I let fear paralyze me, I would have never discovered this hidden gift.

Sometimes you won't know you have a core competency in an area until you try it a few times—even if it seems way outside your comfort zone. If you feel like you don't have many gifts, it may be that you just need to go out there and try some things you haven't done before. Start experimenting with new opportunities and challenges to see what you enjoy and do well. After all, you won't know if you never try. And don't forget to ask others close to you—they can often see your gifts when you're unable to.

TIME CHECK

In order to stay focused on the best things, you need to be sure you are purposefully managing your time. This means you need to map out a regular routine.

I know, I know. This doesn't sound as glamorous as going with the flow and being spontaneous. It might even sound boring to some of you. But until you have a solid idea of how you spend your time—and learn how to do it purposefully—you'll spend your life simply surviving, floundering aimlessly, or worse, stagnating. Routines allow you to get your life in order so you can say goodbye to survival mode and start living your days with purpose.

Most people start their day by thinking about how much time they have and how many tasks, events, appointments, and to-dos they can squeeze in. I've learned it's more effective to start with the most important things in your day. Give those things precedence and priority first, before adding anything else to your schedule. This way, if you only get a few things done in a day's time, you'll have accomplished the few things that matter most.

WHY CAN'T I MAKE THIS WORK?

I didn't always live by this principle. In fact, for years, I thought time management meant trying to find a way to use every possible minute of every day and be as productive as possible. When I started getting overwhelmed and frustrated at my long to-do lists and lack of time, I'd draw a line in the sand and make some hasty declaration like, "From now on, I am going to make a schedule and stick with it!"

My intentions were good, but how I tried to carry them out was not. I was setting myself up for failure from the get-go. In my zeal to be more productive, I'd create an elaborately detailed spreadsheet with what I—and every other person in my household—was supposed to be doing every fifteen minutes of every day.

In theory, this may have been a good idea; but, in practice, it just created more frustration and stress. By trying to micromanage my day—and everyone else's—I'd end up frazzled over any interruption. And that was plain crazy because I have young children. Interruptions and unexpected catastrophes are part of life, especially when you have little ones at home. My first overly regimented attempts at scheduling didn't allow any cushion for inevitable diaper blowouts, phone calls that had to be answered, children who needed extra attention because they were having a difficult day, and impromptu trips to the doctor or emergency room.

Within a few days of creating this overly detailed schedule, I'd crash and burn and end up right back in the middle of chaos and disorder. The problem wasn't the idea of routines; it was trying to cram thirty-two hours' worth of projects into a twenty-four-hour day. No wonder I was exhausted and burned out all the time.

AN ABOUT-FACE

As I mentioned in the first chapter, in 2010, I finally broke down and started hiring help for MoneySavingMom.com. I was overwhelmed and overworked, burning the candle at both ends. I had to either scale back in a big way or bring on some excellent help. One of the first positions I filled was to hire Amy Lynn Andrews (who now runs the popular blogging site, BloggingWithAmy.com) as my virtual assistant.

Amy was a godsend. Not only did she help me streamline many of the business processes that were time-consuming and bogging me down, but she also helped me address an area in my personal life that I was particularly struggling with: managing my personal time.

She encouraged me to stop trying to create these detailed spreadsheet schedules. Instead of listing out the many things I wanted to get done in a day and trying to squeeze them all in, she told me to start with the time I had to work with—twenty-four hours—and then divvy up my responsibilities and priorities into time blocks that fit that time period.

BE INTENTIONAL ABOUT HOW YOU SPEND YOUR TIME

Don't be misled by how simple this method of time management is. It's also very effective. Here's how it works:

1. Add up the hours in a day. (If it's easier for you to track your time on a weekly basis, or 168 hours, do so.)
2. List the activities, tasks, and projects you want to accomplish in that time (e.g., sleep, make meals for the family, work, exercise, volunteer).
3. Divide these activities into a day's time frame.

Here's a sample of one of my days:

- 30 minutes Bible reading/journaling
- 30 minutes one-on-one time with my husband
- 6 hours of homeschooling, playing, and reading with the children
- 30 minutes of exercise
- 30 minutes shower/dress
- 1 hour cleaning/home management
- 7 hours sleeping
- 2 hours meals/meal preparation
- 4 hours blogging/computer work
- 2 hours of extra/margin time

If there's not enough time to do one or more items on your list, Amy suggests that you do the following:

- Steal time from one of your other times.
- Be strategic and creative, and do what you want in less time.
- Delegate the task to someone else.
- Don't do it.

In the space on the next page, create your own time blocks based on a typical day. I know every day will vary to a certain extent, depending on your schedule, but this will give you the foundation from which to build a daily routine.

TIME	ACTIVITY
_____	_____
_____	_____
_____	_____
_____	_____
_____	_____
_____	_____
_____	_____

I am a single, professional mom with four kids, one of whom has special needs. With a child with special needs I have to carefully balance my time. Life is full of kids, work, school, household duties, plus doctor appointments, therapy appointments, medications, sickness, hospitalizations, etc. I keep a planning schedule that includes school, work, and me time. I also put all household activities and chores on it. I keep my time focused on family goals (faith, relaxation, family time, finances). It's not a perfect system, but it does keep me organized and helps with time management.

—ANNA

WHY MARGIN MATTERS

Don't forget to leave some margin room. You'll need this breathing space for when life happens. Like when an unexpected guest knocks at the door, an appointment runs late, your dog throws up all over your couch, or the washer overflows and there's water all over the laundry room floor. You know, life stuff.

You may be tempted to fill up every single waking moment of your day with something, but I heartily encourage you to include two hours of margin time in your budget. Think about it this way. If you schedule in margin and something comes up, your whole day didn't just get blown. You can deal with the interruption, and you'll still have plenty of time to get done everything you need to do. If you don't end up needing any margin, great! Now you've just been given some extra time to use wisely. It's a win-win.

You know what else I love about margin? It means I have time to stop and really enjoy my children and seize teachable moments with them. For instance, last year I discovered a four-foot-long black snake in our backyard. If I didn't have any margin, I probably would have just run on to the next task.

Instead, I called the kids outside, and we spent forty-five minutes observing and taking pictures of the snake. We e-mailed them to Jesse, and he did some research on that slithery creature. When he came home from work, he sat the girls down and gave them an impromptu "lesson" on our backyard visitor. The girls loved it and hung on every word he said.

If our lives were so packed full that we didn't have any margin in them, we would miss out daily on fun opportunities like this one.

MAPPING OUT A REALISTIC ROUTINE

Once you've crafted your time blocks, it's time to create a specific routine. If schedules stress you out, don't worry. This doesn't have to be complicated or overly structured. It doesn't even have to be a minute-by-minute schedule. In fact, unless you really, really want to do that, I encourage you not to. Strict schedules usually set you up for failure—that's why we have margin time. So keep it simple. Once you have a handle on a daily routine, you can get a little more detailed.

I've gleaned a lot of wisdom and inspiration from Marla Cilley, popularly known as "FlyLady" (FlyLady.net). I love many of her concepts. What has helped me the most is her suggestion to have a morning routine and an evening routine. No matter what season of life you're in, you can benefit from implementing both routines in your life.

> He who every morning plans the transaction of the day and follows out the plan, carries a thread that will guide him through the labyrinth of the most busy life.
> —VICTOR HUGO

Here's my current morning routine. I've had one for several years, so mine is a little more than five things. Some items mesh into one another, so I view each line as one thing.

- Get up, read Bible, journal, pray
- Exercise, shower/dress

- Check e-mail, clean out e-mail inbox
- Writing/blogging work
- Breakfast

Once you've consistently stuck with your morning routine for three weeks, add an evening routine for three weeks. At the end of six weeks, you should start to feel some significant order in your life just by following these simple routines.

Here's what my evening routine currently looks like:

- Dinner, read, and pray together as a family
- Clean up the kitchen
- Lay out clothes for the next day
- Wash face, take out contacts, and take vitamins
- Read before bed

If you don't have any structure in your life right now, I encourage you to start with a morning routine. In the space below, write down the five things you need and want to do each morning. Things like exercise, read and pray, clean up the kitchen, wake and feed the kids breakfast, and prepare lunches or even dinner. Whatever those five things are, commit to getting up and doing them consistently for three weeks.

MY MORNING ROUTINE

....

....

....

Put your plan somewhere you can see it, whether on the computer, the refrigerator, or the kitchen counter. It's important to have easy and visible access to it so you can keep track of your time and what you need to do.

> I printed my daily checklist and put it in a frame. It hangs by the kitchen, and I use a dry erase marker to check things off throughout the day. I also try to do that with my weekly cleaning list. I'm not good at vacuuming every Monday, laundry Tuesdays, that kind of thing. So I made a general list. As long as everything gets done throughout the week, it's good for me! But if it's not out in the open where I see it all the time, I won't do it.
> —MEGAN

HOW TO MAKE A ROUTINE WORK FOR YOU

Now it's time to create a routine that works for you. Keep in mind your routine will probably look different on the weekends and to some degree will always be evolving—with a new job, fitness schedule, change of seasons, and so on. Find what works for you and your family, whether it is a detailed, clock-guided schedule, a simple routine, or a customized schedule for each day of the week. The key is to make a plan and follow it until you need to adjust it. Remember, routines don't work unless you work them.

> In truth, people can generally make time for what they choose to do; it is not really the time but the will that is lacking.
> —SIR JOHN LUBBOCK

Get Sleep

Make sleep one of your highest priorities. Some of you may be laughing at this suggestion or even feel frustrated that I'm mentioning it. You may be thinking, *More sleep? Are you kidding me, Crystal? Do you have a clue how many things I have going on? Sleep is always the first thing to go.*

I get it. I've been there and done that. I used to think that burning the midnight oil and getting by on only a fistful of sleep would make me more productive. This is not true! I've found that I'm much more productive if I get at least seven hours of sleep almost every night. Yep, that's right. Almost every night! Truth be told, I try to get eight to nine hours of sleep at least a few times each week (usually on the weekends) as I find this makes me much more energetic and productive throughout the week.

Some people feel that sleep is a waste of time. But when you sleep less, your cognitive processes (like thinking, remembering, paying attention) diminish. Insufficient sleep has been linked to medical and health problems, motor vehicle accidents, industrial disasters, and job mistakes.[2] If you don't get enough sleep, over time you will also be more likely to suffer from depression, chronic diseases like diabetes, and a reduced quality of life and productivity.[3] These are good reasons to hop on the sleep bandwagon!

I'm most productive in the mornings, so I make it a goal to go to bed by ten and get up between five and six. You may be more of a night owl and prefer to stay up late and wake up late. Do whatever works for you. Just aim to get at least seven hours of sleep every night, eight or nine if you can. I guarantee you'll feel better, have more energy, and be more efficient during the day.

If you're in a season of life when it's difficult to get enough sleep (you're working multiple jobs or you have young children), just do the best you can to grab sleep whenever you can get it. Even a fifteen-minute nap in the middle of the day can do wonders!

18 WAYS TO GET A BETTER NIGHT'S SLEEP

1. Get fresh air and sunshine.
2. Take a long soak in a bubble bath before bed.
3. Start winding down early.
4. Turn off electronics at least an hour before bedtime.
5. Go to bed when you start feeling tired (don't wait and catch your second or third wind!).
6. Don't drink caffeine after 3 p.m.

7. Drink Sleepytime Tea (or similar herbal tea) with milk and honey.

8. Use lavender essential oil (spray it on your pillow, dab it on your neck, or rub it on your feet).

9. Write down anything that is keeping you awake.

10. Have a plan for the next day.

11. Go to bed at the same time every night.

12. Make sure your room is cool and dark.

13. Get regular exercise.

14. Dim the lights early.

15. Play soft, soothing music.

16. Get up early (and you'll be tired earlier!).

17. Have white noise in the background.

18. Try earplugs and/or an eye mask.

Get Ruthless

Be tough. Be strong. Be fierce about eliminating the unnecessary items from your to-do list. I think Americans are suffering from a busyness epidemic. We're addicted to busy. So many of us try to find fulfillment and self-worth in piling our plates too high. The busier we are, the more important we feel. This is why our culture, by and large, is exhausted, overworked, and overwhelmed.

So what's the solution? It's really simple, and I've said it already. And I'll keep saying it until you believe me. Just say no.

Stop letting people manipulate you into a miserable existence. Stop doing things just because you feel obligated to do them. Stop doing things because you're afraid of what people might think of you if you don't do them. Stop overcommitting yourself.

> It's not enough to be busy, so are the ants. The question is, what are we busy about?
> —HENRY DAVID THOREAU

Get Help

If you are struggling in a particular area (whether preparing meals, having enough time to work without the support you need, cleaning a constantly dirty house, or accomplishing work-related tasks), don't let pride stand in the way of asking for help. Remember, we can't do it all. And we shouldn't have to.

For years, I felt like I had to do all the tasks of running my business myself because paying someone else to work for me seemed more like a want than a need. However, I finally got to the point where I was working way too many hours and was constantly behind.

You may not need help running your own business, but you may need help in other ways. Maybe you need some childcare in order to accomplish the things on your best stuff list. Consider enlisting the help of a relative, a loved one, or a friend. If you can't afford to pay them, exchange a service for theirs. For example, you might love to cook and your friend may not. Trade her a few meals a week for a few hours of babysitting.

Decorating your home might be an area that suffers because you lack the skill (like I do), and the mere thought of doing it on your own stresses you out. Ask a talented friend who loves interior design to give you some pointers. It will save you time and aggravation. And your friend will probably be thrilled that you asked for her input.

HELP FOR THE SINGLE MOM

I can only imagine how hard it is to be a single mom. It can be difficult enough raising children in a two-parent home. Single moms have unique challenges that need to be addressed. Here is a comment from Susan, who offers some great tips:

I'm a single, working mom. With nine to ten hours a day working/commuting plus seven to eight hours of sleep, there's not much time left over to maintain the household and raise my child. It's tough. My only regular "me time" is early mornings. Every now and then I can nab some computer or personal time in the evenings, but I cannot ever count on it.

Here are some things that help:

1. If possible, pay for outside help. My four magic words are "yard guy" and "cleaning lady." It's not a luxury; for me, it's a necessity. You can't put a price on your sanity.

2. Do what you can on your lunch hour. Every other Friday (which corresponds, not accidentally, to my paydays), I sit at my desk at work, review my finances, and pay my bills. With the ability to pay bills online nowadays, it's convenient if you have a computer in front of you and some privacy. (If your employer restricts personal use of computers, use your own laptop.)

3. I don't do this in the hotter months, but when the weather is colder, it easier to shop at lunchtime and leave groceries in the car. If you

have a fridge at work, use it to store your colder items until you go home.

4. If possible, take time off from work for "me time." I take a personal day every now and then to do some things I wouldn't ordinarily have time to do, like Christmas shopping. When I'm feeling particularly rundown, I'll take a day off to sleep. I think it's especially important to do this if you're sick.

Great advice, Susan! Here are more helpful tips that might save you time as a single mom.

- Double up on tasks. Multitasking can sometimes be a woman's best friend. When your kids are in the tub, clean the bathroom, wash your face, brush your teeth, and wipe down the counters.
- Simplify your mornings by getting things ready the night before (what you and your kids will wear, eat, and need for the day).
- Use the Internet to your advantage. Being online is not always a bad thing or a time sucker. If you are diligent with how you use the web, you can save a ton of time. Shop online, connect with friends and family, manage your finances and health through online trackers, and make appointments.

Get Efficient

If you want to be more productive, you need to become the master of your minutes. Do you have short five-minute windows of time here and there? Don't just twiddle your thumbs, mindlessly browse the web, or check your Facebook news feed for the tenth time today. Do something productive.

I'm always surprised at how much can be accomplished in a few minutes of time. For example, you can do the following:

- Write a thank-you note or encouraging e-mail.
- Clean the kitchen sink or bathroom toilet.
- Switch a load of laundry from the washer to the dryer.
- Pull out dinner from the freezer.
- Make a healthy snack to munch on instead of grazing on high-calorie, low-nutrition foods.
- Take your vitamins, and drink a glass of water.
- Do twenty-five sit-ups.
- Tidy up a room.
- Read a short story to your child.
- Wipe down the kitchen counters.
- Text your husband to tell him you love him.
- Read two pages of the book you're currently reading.
- Pray for someone you know who is struggling or for a need in your own life.

There are a thousand other ideas for how to use wisely the little slots of time that pop up throughout the day. Don't let these golden nuggets slip by unproductively. They can quickly add up in your favor.

> Don't be stomping on ants when you have elephants to feed.
> —PETER TURLA

NEED SOME MORE IDEAS ON HOW TO SAVE TIME?

The following tips are invaluable whether you are single, a working mom, a stay-at-home mom, or just plain busy!

Do a dinner swap. Get a group of three or four girlfriends or family members and have each person cook a quadruple meal each week to share with one another.

If you have children, get them to help out. If they are old enough to pull out a toy, they are old enough to put it back. Don't do everything yourself. Share the load.

Stick with one shopping trip a week. Instead of making multiple trips to different stores during the week, try doing them all in one afternoon.

If certain projects, to-dos, and tasks can wait, let them wait. Do them on days that are not as busy or schedule-oriented, perhaps on the weekends.

Use lists. Chapter 6 offers detailed information on creating daily goal sheets and tasks. Lists can be used to plan meals, organize your day, pack for getaways, and figure out your schedule.

Multitask. Walk the dog, and get in a power walk. Make a phone call while cleaning up the kitchen. Empty or load the dishwasher while waiting for water to boil.

Mix chores and play. Feel like watching a movie? Do some ironing, exercise, or fold laundry while being entertained.

WHAT YOU WANT TO KNOW ▮▮▮▮▮▮▮▮▮▮▮▮▮▮▮▮▮▮

Q: I'm excited about the new routine I've created, but I'm scared that my family isn't going to be too thrilled about it. How do I get them on board with the plan I've created?

A: First off, the worst thing you can do is take your new routine and start barking orders at everyone. I promise that's only going to make your troops want to rebel!

Instead, call a family meeting—or whatever it is that you do at your house when breaking big news—and enthusiastically let them know that you've got some great ideas for summer you want to talk to them about. You set the tone for how they are going to receive the changes, and your excitement will invariably be contagious.

Share some of your ideas and then ask for their input. Listen to them, and take their suggestions to heart. Your plan is a great starting place, but it's by no means set in stone. In fact, I encourage you to make some adjustments to it based on the input of your family. They probably have some great ideas you wouldn't have thought of on your own.

Once you've all signed off on your plan of action, make sure that everyone clearly knows how it's going to work and what is expected of them. If a routine is something new to your kids, review and practice how it's supposed to go. Don't expect that they'll know how to follow a list or complete a project if you haven't shown them how.

And don't be discouraged if it takes awhile for the new routine to stick or if you end up needing to tweak it after a few days. That's totally okay!

Be Flexible

Your routines do not own or master you. They are simply guidelines to help you. If your children or husband need some extra time from you or something important comes up that doesn't coincide with your plan, press the Pause button and come back to it when you can.

For instance, if my children are intently working together on a project, I might let them continue with what they are working on and use that time to do some cleaning, which was scheduled for a different time during the day. Then I'll skip or condense the cleaning and playtime in the afternoon and use that extra time for something else.

The purpose of a routine is to benefit you and your family. It's not an excuse to bulldoze everyone over. And remember, if something in your routine isn't helping your family, it needs to be tweaked or changed.

Before you dive in to the next chapter, do yourself a favor and figure out your best stuff list, map out your time blocks for the twenty-four hours in your day, and then determine what you're going to cut and cull from your current schedule and responsibility list. While this exercise will take some effort, I promise that it will be worth it to simplify your life so you no longer spend your days being busy with little to show for it but exhaustion. Instead, put forth the work now so you become the

master of your minutes and start being in control of your day—
and ultimately your life!

▮▮▮▮▮▮▮▮▮▮ GET PRACTICAL ▮▮▮▮▮▮▮▮▮▮▮

Track your time. You may not have time because you're
not managing it well. Keep a detailed time log of what
you do every thirty minutes during a two- to three-day
period to see where the twenty-four hours of each day
are going. This exercise will invariably be enlightening
and possibly disheartening when you realize how much
time is being wasted or spent carelessly. Don't be
discouraged if you are unhappy with what you see. Use
the information gleaned to make positive changes.

Evaluate your activities. Evaluate all the activities and
commitments on your plate right now. Choose one that
really doesn't matter or doesn't revolve around your best
stuff list. Then get rid of it. If it's something that involves
other people, make sure you don't walk out on them
without tying up all the loose ends first.

Let it go. Say goodbye to anything that is not the best
right now. Just do it! I know you can, no matter how hard
it might seem. You'll thank me later!

3

If You Aim at Nothing, You'll Hit It Every Time

> CAT: Where are you going?
> ALICE: Which way should I go?
> CAT: That depends on where you are going.
> ALICE: I don't know.
> CAT: Then it doesn't matter which way you go.
> —LEWIS CARROLL, *ALICE IN WONDERLAND*

Goal: Find purpose and motivation through goal setting.

Strategy: Set specific, measurable, and realistic goals, break them down into bite-size pieces, and then develop a plan of action to follow through with them.

"Crystal, I have to tell you something," my friend Jenae excitedly told me at a blogging event we attended together. I had no idea where she was headed with this conversation, but I could tell it was going to be good.

Jenae, a former teacher turned stay-at-home mom of two boys, shared with me how she'd never set goals. But after reading my blog and learning about the importance of goal setting, she decided to try it. She said she was amazed at the difference it had made in her life.

Prior to this, Jenae was living mostly in survival mode. It seemed all she was doing was making sure everyone stayed fed, dressed, and well cared for. That was her existence in a nutshell.

When Jenae started setting little goals, she couldn't believe how much more purpose she had in life. No longer was she just getting up and trying to make it through the day. Rather, she was waking up with purpose. Here's what Jenae has learned through this process:

Unless I am truly passionate about something, I struggle immensely with the self-discipline needed to perform the task. Unfortunately, exercise, healthy eating, and cleaning don't rank very high on my list of passions. As a mom of two young boys, I am completely drained of energy by the end of each day and adding anything extra seems unbearable.

In January 2012, I implemented many of Crystal's goal-setting tips for the New Year. My goals were quite simple, but accomplishing them made a huge difference. Some of them included:

- Go to bed with the sink empty and the countertops wiped down every night.
- Eat a home-cooked dinner around the kitchen table with the entire family at least four times each week.
- Go on at least one date night with my husband each month.
- Spend thirty minutes playing with the boys each day.

Writing down these goals and breaking them into smaller steps made it much easier and more motivating for me to accomplish the mundane tasks (like laundry, cleaning, organizing, daily grind–type things) day after day and week after week.

It would be dishonest for me to say that I have stuck with all the goals I have made for myself (have I mentioned that I have issues following through with things as well?). However, I was able to meet the ones above, which was a huge improvement for me!

Setting goals, writing them down, and achieving them has given me a renewed sense of purpose and fulfillment. As for the ones that haven't yet been reached (like losing those five extra pounds), I am thankful that tomorrow is a new day and I have a plan of action to tackle these stubborn issues!

Goal setting gave Jenae drive, momentum, and meaning she never knew was possible as a stay-at-home mom. The same can happen to you, no matter what season or stage of life you're in.

THE POWER OF GOAL SETTING

We only have one life to live. In order to make the most of it and live intentionally and purposefully, we have to constantly reevaluate our lives. Creating and monitoring short-term and long-term goals is a life-changing way to make sure we are heading in the right direction.

> If you're bored with life, if you don't get up every morning with a burning desire to do things, you don't have enough goals.
>
> —LOU HOLTZ

My friend Anne, who blogs at ModernMrsDarcy.com, shared with me the amazing results of goal setting that she and her family experienced in the area of their finances. Here's what she has to say:

Last January my husband and I set an ambitious goal to pay off a loan with a hefty balance, about half our annual income, within two years' time. This goal was important but not at all fun, and we had a hard time getting ourselves to even set it in the first place. But we knew we had to do it so we could move on to more exciting financial goals. So we committed ourselves to slogging it out.

Right at the beginning of the year, we scored some small successes that skyrocketed our hopes for reaching our goal. I filled in at work for a sick coworker and worked several forty-hour weeks instead of my usual ten. We received a larger-than-expected tax refund and a birthday check or two. All of a sudden, we were making real progress. Our goal began to look achievable.

At that point, we started throwing everything we had at that loan balance: income from a side gig, three-dollar rebate checks, spare change, birthday money. You name it; it all went toward the loan. We kept a running tally of the loan balance by the computer where we worked. As December neared, we couldn't believe how close we were getting to a zero balance. We started to wonder if we could pull it off in one year's time. Sure enough, I got a Christmas bonus at work, and we received a few Christmas checks, which made us able to pay off that loan just before the New Year. We were thrilled!

I learned so much about goal setting from that experience. I learned not to be afraid to set big goals—we never would have paid off that balance in a year if we hadn't aimed high. I also learned I can create my own momentum. Even though I wasn't at all excited about setting that (boring, no-fun) goal, I found that working toward it increased my enthusiasm. And the experience continues to inspire me to aim high and dream big.

SET SMART GOALS

Goals aren't just dreams, wishful thinking, or lofty ambitions. They must be SMART—specific, measurable, attainable, realistic, and time-bound—blueprints to get you where you want to go. Using these SMART principles will help you create goals you can achieve. If you don't know where you're aiming, you're going to lack direction and purpose.

Specific

Goals aren't meant to be vague or ambiguous. Though you may genuinely want to "have a better life," "get healthier," or "become rich," those are merely undefined intentions. They won't get you anywhere. You have to identify the details of your goals. For example, instead of saying, "I want to lose weight," make a goal to lose five pounds in four weeks. Or instead of saying, "I want to save money this year," say, "I want to save five hundred dollars every month for twelve months."

Measurable

You need to be able to track your progress in order to see your desired result. Your goal must answer the question: How will I know if I reached my goal? For example, if you want to write a book, a measurable goal is to complete one chapter a month.

Attainable

Your goals must be within your control and influence and mean something to you. Don't commit yourself to reaching a goal that you won't be able to attain. I'm not seeking to become a world-class traveler, an Olympic swimmer, or an inventor right now (and probably won't in the near or distant future!), so none of my goals are going to push me closer to those things. We must choose goals that relate to our life priorities.

Realistic

There's a big difference between shooting for the moon and meeting a realistic goal. Your goals should stretch and challenge you as a person, but not be so difficult or ambitious that you have little to no chance of meeting them. For instance, it's pretty unrealistic to get your master's degree in a year's time if you already have a stressful and time-consuming job and a family. You'll be better off setting a goal to meet that education achievement in two to three years.

Time-Bound

Your goals must have an end date. If they don't, you will be less likely to meet them. Consider how much time you think it will take to accomplish your goal and then set a date by which to have it completed. It's not enough to set a goal to read more self-improvement books. Make it time-bound by writing down ten specific self-improvement titles you plan to read over the next ten months.

Don't worry too much about being locked in to a particular date, though. You can always change it if you need to, but the act of setting a date will give you much more momentum and drive. And you just might pick up speed the closer you get to the finish line.

> Whenever you want to achieve something, keep your eyes open, concentrate and make sure you know exactly what it is you want. No one can hit their target with their eyes closed.
> —PAULO COELHO

WHAT KIND OF GOALS ARE WE TALKING ABOUT?

You may have some idea of what goals you'd like to reach, or you may feel so swamped with life that you haven't given thought to making any—other than trying to get through the day. If that's where you are, I encourage you to start with a few small goals.

I like to break down my goals into different categories. Following are some examples you can work from. You can pick and choose from this list, create your own, or do a little of both.

- Business
- Personal
- Health/Nutrition/Fitness
- Financial
- Marriage
- Family/Parenting
- Home management
- Education

In the space below or in a separate journal or notebook, write down four or five categories where you'd like to see changes in your life. Then figure out what you want to accomplish in these areas.

....

....

....

....

....

Here are some examples of SMART goals to get the idea wheels turning in your brain:

Business
- Create a website for my business within the next six months.
- Set up a blog on my website, and update it at least once or twice a week.

- Find a mentor (either online or in my local area) this month, and set up biweekly meetings with him or her.

Personal

- Have a consistent sleep schedule, and get seven hours of rest every night.
- Learn Spanish by spending an hour a day listening to lessons on my iPod.
- Start a family scrapbook, and update it every month.

Health/Nutrition/Fitness

- Run a two-mile race in the fall of this year.
- Drink eight glasses of water each day, and limit soda intake to twice each week.
- Lose twenty pounds in four months by eating less and exercising more.

To guide you even further, I thought you might like to get a peek at what some of my yearly goals look like. This is a list of some of the goals I set for 2012:

Personal

- Read the twenty-four books on my booklist.
- Read the Bible in a year.
- Run in one 5K race.

Marriage

- Go on at least two overnight trips as a couple (without our kids).
- Have monthly date nights.
- Read three books on marriage.

Family/Parenting

- Memorize two or three Bible verses with the children each month.
- Enroll our children in ice-skating and swimming lessons.
- Read fifteen books aloud together as a family.

Financial

- Save up and pay cash for a new-to-us vehicle to replace our family van.
- Tithe 10 percent of our income.

If you're new to setting goals, keep it simple, and start with a few goals. It's much better to set two goals and work hard and finish them than to set thirty-two goals and be so overwhelmed that you don't make progress on any of them.

GOAL-SETTING SUCCESS

Over the years, I've learned a lot about the art of goal setting and what really works. Two things that I've found to be imperative to goal-setting success are writing down your goals and breaking them down into bite-size pieces.

> By recording your dreams and goals on paper, you set in motion the process of becoming the person you most want to be.
> —MARK VICTOR HANSEN

Write It Down

Goals that you say out loud or think of are a good start, but you need to take your intentions a step further. Write them down. Seeing your goal written in ink, on paper, will have a powerful effect on your mind.

I love how Dave Ramsey encourages people to put their financial goals on paper and on purpose. When you write down your goals, it puts more weight to them. It also gives you a start date. When you have a start date, you are motivated to actually, you know, start. Plus, if you write your goals down, you're able to track your progress and be encouraged by advancing in the right direction.

You can download a free, printable goal-setting worksheet on MoneySavingMom.com (search for "goal-planning sheet," and see a sample in the appendix) or find one elsewhere that works for you. If you prefer a simpler method of writing down goals than using a worksheet, by all means go for it. A sticky note taped to your mirror or refrigerator or a reminder set up on your phone may work just as well. There is no right way to write down goals. The point is to get your goals in print so you can follow through with them.

> I'm trying to steer clear of electronic planning. Things feel more real to me when put on paper. If I physically write something, I seem to remember it better.
> —ALICIA

One more thing: put your goals somewhere you can see them. You want to be able to look at your goals on a regular basis to remind yourself of your target. Remember, out of sight, out of mind. And that's not what you want when it comes to making and meeting your goals.

THREE METHODS TO WRITE DOWN YOUR GOALS

1. **Create a list.** How you write down your goals will depend on your preference. I like to type up my weekly, monthly, and yearly goal lists and then cross them off as I finish them. There's something about putting a line through a goal to mark it as completed that gives me immense satisfaction.
2. **Design a spreadsheet.** Typing my goals and crossing them off is very motivating to me. Other people (like my husband) prefer to create a sophisticated spreadsheet to track the percentage of progress for each goal. When we were saving to buy our home, Jesse set up an Excel spreadsheet with our end house savings goals and our monthly house savings goals. Each month he'd input how much we'd saved into the spreadsheet, and it would automatically update our savings percentages. This method inspired him.
3. **Use sticky notes.** If you're a visual person and need a lot of reminders, try using sticky notes. Place them throughout your house where they will help you remember to stay on track. Here is what this could look like in your home:

   - Aiming to lose five pounds? Put sticky notes on the fridge and pantry reminding you to choose your foods wisely.
   - Training for your first 5K race? Put a sticky note on your

laptop reminding you to go for a run before you open your computer.

- Seeking to increase your blog profitability? Put a sticky note on your computer reminding you to stop wasting time on Facebook.
- Wanting to become more organized with your meal planning? Put a sticky note on your bathroom mirror reminding you to take out meat to defrost while you're brushing your teeth before bed.

Instead of just dreaming up big ideas or fantasizing about lofty ambitions, take the first step to success today by writing down your goals.

Break Down Your Goal

Once you've written down some goals, develop an incremental plan of action. Some goals require baby steps while others can be tackled head-on, with only one or two action steps. For instance, a goal to save five thousand dollars in one year will require daily or weekly goals like limiting spending, clipping coupons, and so on. A simple goal to start taking vitamins regularly won't require anything except picking a time to take them on a daily basis and then just doing it. (Set an alarm on your phone or put a sticky note on your bathroom mirror to remind you!)

When you take the time to break down a goal into smaller chunks, it looks doable rather than overwhelming. It's easier to stay focused if you are only looking at the next few steps ahead of you than the huge mountain you're aiming to climb. Map your small steps and then take them. Before you know it, you'll be at the summit.

Trying to lose fifty pounds can be daunting unless you break it down and focus on losing one half or full pound a week. Successful marathoners can't get hung up worrying about how they are going to finish the twenty-six-mile race; they have to pace themselves for the mile or half mile that they are currently running. You may feel going back to school and getting your degree is impossible until you take one semester or class at a time. If you have a home piled with clutter, you won't be able to overhaul it in a day. If, however, you set a timer for fifteen minutes every day (more on this principle later) and work faithfully on it for three months, you'll see some real progress.

Here are two sample plans, one for a short-term goal and one for a long-term goal. I've broken down both goals into smaller chunks to give you an idea of how this works.

How to Train for a 5K in Twelve Weeks

- Sign up for a 5K race scheduled sometime in the next three to four months.
- Find someone to train with you or hold you accountable, if possible.
- Download the Couch to 5K app or print out a copy of the program.
- Decide when and where you will run (outside, at home on a treadmill, at the gym) and how you will accomplish it in the midst of your busy schedule.
- Make a chart on your phone or stick one on the fridge for you to track your progress. Write at the top "I Will Run a 5K on _____." Choose a big reward that you'll earn if you accomplish this goal.

- Check in with your accountability partner after every run, either via e-mail, text, phone, or in person. If it helps, consider posting your run times online via your Facebook status. The more accountability, the better!
- Reward yourself with something small every week to help you stick with your plan.
- After you've run the 5K, enjoy the fulfillment of a job well done and the reward you listed earlier.
- Set your next fitness goal!

How to Pay Off $5,000 in Debt This Year

- Call a family meeting to discuss your desire to pay off this debt and why. Make sure everyone is onboard.
- Create a spreadsheet to detail your monthly and weekly goals. (If you want to pay off $5,000 in twelve months, you'll need to pay off $416.67 each month, or $96.15 each week, or $13.70 per day.)
- Brainstorm as a family specific things you are going to cut from your budget each month and week to achieve these goals. If possible, rotate the different things you cut each month to provide some variety and prevent feelings of deprivation.
- Discuss ways you could increase your income to be able to pay off the debt faster.
- Decide on a specific reward you'll get every month if you achieve the monthly goal.
- Pick a reward for the whole family if you end up meeting your ultimate goal.

- Track your weekly progress on your spreadsheet or on your fridge.
- Schedule monthly accountability meetings to make sure you're staying on track, to tweak your budget, and to talk about what's working and what's not working.

> Desires must be simple and definite. They defeat their own purpose should they be too many, too confusing, or beyond a man's training to accomplish.
> —GEORGE S. CLASON

HOW TO STAY ON THE WAGON AND MEET YOUR GOALS

It's easy to get excited when you first start planning goals. You can probably even stretch your momentum over a period of a few weeks. Fueled by passion and enthusiasm, you count calories with a vengeance. You study long and hard. You stick to your exercise regimen like white on rice. You clip coupons like you're Edward Scissorhands.

But then something happens.

Your efforts slow down. Life happens. Distractions pop up. You eat a piece of cake and figure another slice wouldn't hurt. You have to take your mom to her doctor's appointment, so you miss a study session (or two). You get sick and are unable to exercise. A work deadline causes you to put your blog schedule on hold. Sometimes you just lose your motivation and before you know it, so much time has passed you can't even remember what your goals were in the first place.

While discouragement, detours, or setbacks will happen along the way, they don't have to totally derail your efforts in achieving your goals. Here are some simple ways to help stay or get back on track, even when you have to press the Pause button momentarily.

Have Realistic Expectations

Simply put, don't bite off more than you can chew. One of the biggest reasons I was a goal-setting failure for so long was because I would set far too many goals. Most of them were great; I just had too many. If I were to attempt the impossible and pull off all the goals, I wouldn't have much time left over for anything else, including sleep!

> I signed up to take some college courses awhile back. Recently, I dealt with some serious personal problems, so I had to drop a class. I felt like a failure at first, but realized it was better to focus on and do the best in the classes I could manage than do poorly in all of them. It was a great learning lesson.
>
> —JENNIFER

Not long ago, my husband was going through some papers in our basement and came across the goals we had written down for 2007. It was amazing to see how much I've grown in the area of goal setting since then. Some of the goals were doable and realistic (and ones that I actually achieved). But most of them were impossible and wholly out of line with the SMART principles.

Guess how many goals were on that list. Thirty-seven! I kid you not. Did I mention at the time I had a three-year-old and a baby, was running two online businesses, and I didn't have any local help with childcare or the websites? Some of these goals were completely unrealistic for me at that season of life. They included things like "Get up at 5 a.m. every day" (hello, I was getting up multiple times a night with a baby!) and "Read one to two books every week." It was simply absurd for me to think I could accomplish all thirty-seven goals that year with everything else on my plate.

I'm a firm believer in aiming high and challenging yourself to always be learning, growing, and improving as a person. That's why goal setting is so important to me. However, it's just as important to be realistic. You need to consider the constraints on your time, your current family and work responsibilities, your energy levels, the ages of your children, and so forth. For instance, a mom of three young children, one of whom has special needs, should have a much different level of expectation for herself than a woman who is young, single, and has no kids.

> Setting goals for your game is an art. The trick is in setting them at the right level neither too low nor too high.
> —GREG NORMAN

It's better to set microscopic goals and make headway on them than to set goals so far out of your reach that you give up before you even begin. When you're first starting out, keep your goals simple and doable. As you start accomplishing them and have a better understanding of what it takes to achieve them, you can set your sights higher.

Review, Tweak, and Repeat

Post your goals where you can see them, and review your progress regularly—at least once a month, if not weekly. I set yearly goals and break these down into monthly goals. Then I break these down even further into weekly goals.

For instance, I chose forty-eight book titles I planned to read this year. Then I broke down this list further by assigning four books to each month of the year. I set a reading goal for each week (reading eight to ten chapters of two different books) to keep me on track.

At the end of each week, I take some time to review last week's goals and map out goals in each category for the following week. I then tentatively assign each of these tasks to specific days during the following week. This exercise usually only takes me fifteen minutes to do, but it makes a world of difference in my week.

> As an adult, I find it hard to be accountable to someone else. It's my life. Why should I need to answer to anyone else? But it's also why I struggle with accomplishing my goals. As it turns out, I really need someone to help me stay focused and grounded.
> —CAMERON

If you are struggling with feeling overwhelmed in the goals you have set for yourself, step back and reevaluate. Do you need to tweak your goals a little to be more realistic? Do you need to give yourself more time to get them done? Sometimes situations come up outside your control and you need to adjust your goals accordingly.

Be Accountable

Reaching our goals is easier and more encouraging when we have people in our lives who will hold us accountable, challenge us, and cheer us on. Whenever I run alone, I tend to go easier on myself. If my side starts hurting or I have a long to-do list, I use that as an excuse for a short run. However, when I run with someone else, I'm motivated to push a little harder, go a little faster, and not give up when I feel winded and tired.

It's the same with life. When you feel like you're going at it alone, it's harder to keep on when the going gets rough. But when you have others around you who are encouraging you, checking on you, or texting you to make sure you're following through, you're much more apt to stick with your goals.

I've found accountability to be key in helping me to stay on track with my goals. I blog about my goals at the beginning of each year and then post my progress at the end of each month. It's amazing how much this practice has helped to keep me on track. If I don't stick with my goals, I have to give an explanation to my entire blog audience!

In addition, my husband and I keep each other accountable when it comes to staying on track with our financial goals. On a regular basis, we talk about big purchases we need to make and discuss the details of our budget.

When I was working on getting up early each morning, my friend Stacie and I texted each other as soon as we got up in the morning. Knowing I was accountable to her and vice versa helped me make sure I didn't go back to sleep.

You might be thinking, *I wish I had an accountability partner, but I don't know where to find one.* Well, it might not be as hard as you think. Anyone can be your accountability partner—your husband, parent, sibling, friend, or neighbor. Start with your local friends and family, and see if anyone would be interested in keeping you accountable to one specific goal. Plan regular accountability meetings, such as meeting for coffee once a month or as many times as you'd like to discuss the progress of your goals.

If you can't find anyone locally, ask friends on Facebook, Twitter, your blog, or other online groups you're a part of. Or search and see if there's already an online support group of some sort. You could even create a chart to track your progress and post it on your fridge at home or cubicle wall at work for everyone to see. The public accountability might be just the motivation you need.

What to Look for in an Accountability Partner

When looking for an accountability partner, find someone who is encouraging, committed, and not afraid to tell you the truth if you're getting behind or offtrack. He or she needs to be willing and able to take you to task if you're not following through with the goals you've set. At the same time, you want someone who will give you grace and understanding when you've set the bar too high or when unexpected situations outside your control come up.

WHAT YOU WANT TO KNOW ▪▪▪▪▪▪▪▪▪▪▪▪▪▪

Q: I have learned so much from you about goal setting, but I'm finding myself getting overly obsessive about reaching my goals, and I feel terrible if I haven't been able to cross off all my little bite-sized pieces of my goals at the end of the day. I almost feel like I want to give up my goals so I stop being so obsessed. Please help me find a better balance! —Lena

A: I really appreciate you asking this question. While I'm a big fan of goal setting, I think it's imperative that we not go overboard with them so that they control our lives—ultimately sucking the joy of living out of life itself.

Goals are meant to be a blessing, not a burden. The reason you set goals is to enhance your life, not to exhaust and overburden you. If goals become additional stress in your life, they need to be tweaked, rewritten, or dropped altogether.

It's good to challenge ourselves. It's good to push ourselves outside our comfort zones. It's good to aim high and work hard. But there always needs to be room to breathe in life. Charging ahead at breakneck speed just for the sake of speed and productivity is no way to live.

With this in mind, here are five ideas for you to consider trying:

1. Create weekly goals versus daily goals. I always encourage people to break their goals down into bite-sized pieces, because viewing a big goal in one lump sum can be overwhelming.

However, if you break a goal down so small that you feel obligated to always be working on it *every single day*—even when the inevitable interruptions come up— you can end up feeling like you've failed or fallen way behind when you don't hit your daily goals.

Perhaps a better option for you would be to choose a few small, bite-sized goals to tackle each week versus each day. Write them down, and post them on your refrigerator or somewhere else that you'll see regularly and then fit them in as you're able throughout the week.

This way, you are still chipping away at your goals, but you're doing so in a way that's more flexible and adaptable to your schedule. On days that you're really busy, you can just focus on the basics. On days that you have some extra time, you can knock out one or two of the bite-sized pieces.

If you don't get to all the short list of goals that week, bump the leftovers to the following week.

2. Make your goals your first priority of the day. In the past year, I've been making a very concerted effort to do the hardest things first. This means I'm starting the day by tackling some of my least favorite but most important tasks first.

Truthfully, this is making a *world* of difference for me. I realized that I'd been wasting a lot of time just stalling.

I'd add things to tomorrow's to-do list or file things to do later instead of doing it now. There's a time and place for filing and putting things on tomorrow's to-do list, but I've been challenging myself to stop procrastinating on these things and face them head-on.

Not only am I getting a lot more done, I'm also finding I have a lot more margin time. Because once you stop stalling and start working, it takes a whole lot less time to do things!

3. Take a day off once a week. If you go-go-go all week long and never take a break, you're bound to burn yourself out. Give yourself at least one day off each week that you don't worry about work, goals, or to-do lists. This is your day to refuel and refresh.

We have Sundays set aside as our day off at our house. We go to church, come home and have a really simple lunch, and then have a quiet afternoon resting, reading, talking, playing a game, or engaging in other relaxing activities.

I don't blog or worry about business stuff or goals, and I often don't even turn on my phone or computer all day long. It's a day we look forward to all week!

If you can't take a full day off, at least take half a day every week. I promise that you'll find you are more productive when you take time to recharge than if you keep going and never stop to take a breath.

4. Set fewer goals. Experiment with lowering the bar a little when it comes to goal setting. Maybe what you're getting hung up on is the fact that you're trying to accomplish too many goals.

It's better to have fewer goals and follow through with them than to have a lot of goals and end up overwhelmed by them. Go through your goal list and try culling it down to the most important goals for four to six weeks. Just focus on those, and see if that makes a difference in your stress level.

5. Give yourself grace. You're pretty much never going to get everything done that you want to in a day's time. That's just life! Focus on what you have accomplished instead of beating yourself up over what you didn't accomplish.

If you end the day feeling like you accomplished nowhere near what you'd hoped, don't fret. Just transfer the things you didn't get done to tomorrow's to-do list (or decide to skip them altogether), go to bed, get some rest, and wake up to a new day tomorrow!

ALL YOU NEED IS FIFTEEN MINUTES A DAY

Do you want to start goal setting but it feels overwhelming to you? Well, never fear, I have an idea that will help inch your way toward whatever your goal is. In fact, this principle can positively change your life. It can be applied to any project you want to accomplish or a goal you want to achieve. It's so simple, but it really works!

All you need to work on your goals is fifteen minutes. No matter how busy your schedule, there is likely something you could give up somewhere to carve out this small amount of time each day.

Here are some fifteen-minute time wasters you can decrease or eliminate altogether to help get you started:

- Hitting the snooze button when the first alarm sounds.
- Browsing the web.
- Being nosy on Facebook and browsing through other people's profiles.
- Spending too much time on any kind of social media.
- Chatting on the phone about nothing with someone you just talked to a few hours earlier.
- Watching TV.
- Shopping for another pair of black shoes when you already own a few pairs.

While it might seem like fifteen minutes isn't much, investing this time every day on a consistent basis can really start to add up to significant traction made and ground covered.

> Take care of the minutes and the hours will take care of themselves.
> —LORD CHESTERFIELD

Think about it this way. Fifteen minutes a day adds up to

- 105 minutes (or 1 hour and 45 minutes) each week,

- almost a full day's worth of work (7.5 hours) put in over a month's time, and
- 90 hours a year! Ninety hours of focused work on your goals list will certainly get you somewhere, don't you think?

Here's an idea. Start using the fifteen-minute principle by making a prioritized list of the things you want to accomplish in the order you want to get them done. Set a timer for fifteen minutes every morning. (I use Online-Stopwatch.com or the timer on my smartphone.) Begin chipping away at this list until the timer goes off. If possible, do this early in the day—before breakfast and the daily hustle and bustle. You may prefer to focus on only one or two goals.

Here are just a few things you can accomplish within that fifteen-minute time frame:

- If your goal is to lose weight, you can exercise or make a healthy meal.
- If your goal is to read more, you can read a few chapters in a book (depending on how long they are, of course).
- If your goal is to save money, you can research coupon deals for the week, work on your budget, or look for ways to supplement your income.
- If your goal is to get certified in a particular field of interest, you can study for an exam.
- If you want to learn a new language, you can listen to an instructional CD.
- If you want to write a book, you can write a few paragraphs a day.

THE EARLY BIRD GETS THE WORM

Getting up early and working for thirty minutes or an hour while the rest of the world sleeps is one of the most efficient and simplest ways to make great strides toward your goals. This effective habit is what spurred my public commitment to develop self-discipline.

Sure, when the alarm clock goes off early in the morning, another hour of sleep sounds so much better than tackling a project. But I guarantee that if you faithfully get up and put in that hour or more of work, it can pay off big-time.

This is how I wrote my first book. With three young children, I knew that I didn't have much extra time in the middle of the day for writing. So I started going to bed between 8 and 9 p.m. and getting up at 4 a.m. almost every weekday for an extra hour of uninterrupted time to write in the morning.

I don't know how I did it some days, dragging every ounce of my tired body out of my warm and cozy bed. But when the book was finished, I knew it was worth it to rearrange my schedule and get up earlier. There were plenty of days when I really, really wanted to go back to sleep and had a long list of excuses why it was okay for me to sleep in. But I made myself get up.

Getting up early is not rocket science. You just have to do it. If this is an area you'd like to work on, here are some helpful suggestions that have worked for me:

- Go to bed an hour or two earlier than you usually do.
- Start winding down at least an hour before you plan to go to bed.
- Buy an alarm without a snooze button.

- Set multiple alarms in your room.
- Have a friend give you a wake-up call.
- Make yourself do it. When your alarm sounds in the morning, get up right then, and jump in the shower to wake yourself up. Or put on your shoes and go for a morning run (a great way to squeeze in some exercise). Even if you're dog-tired, you'll probably feel wide-awake by the time you get home. One friend of mine sticks her face in front of the freezer for a few seconds to help wake up. The cold blast of air really helps her eyes to stay open!

FOCUSED INTENSITY IS KEY

While you can accomplish more than you think in just fifteen minutes a day, it's still not a lot of time. Devote all your attention to your goal during that short time frame. You can't afford to lose even one minute.

Depending on what your task is, I recommend setting up an area in your home with whatever supplies or materials you need during this time (laptop, notebook, writing materials, research, etc.). You want to be ready to dive in to your task without wasting any time.

> Concentrate all your thoughts upon the work at hand. The sun's rays do not burn until brought to a focus.
> —ALEXANDER GRAHAM BELL

Remove all distractions, and don't let anything deter you from your purpose during those fifteen minutes. Turn off your phone, TV, and laptop (if you're not using it). Make sure no one is around. Settle into a quiet space, and get done what you need to get done.

If you have a husband or children, you may have to do this in the morning when everyone is sleeping or when your kids are in school or during their naps. You may feel it's better for you to spend this time at night, when everyone is in bed. Do what works for you.

Stick with your fifteen-minute-per-day commitment and I promise, slowly but surely, you'll start to see results. I have a feeling you'll be amazed at how much you can accomplish when you work with such focused intensity. Not only does such a short window of time discourage you from wasting that time or procrastinating, but you also won't struggle with running out of steam because your time will be up before you know it!

AIM HIGH

I've talked a lot about setting realistic, attainable goals, especially if you are new to goal setting. I also want to encourage you to reach for the stars. Don't be afraid of setting goals that may seem out of reach. I'm not talking about goals that are not in line with your priorities, natural abilities, or God-given talents. I'm talking about goals that will take a lot of hard work, sacrifice, and big prayers.

I'm reminded of my friend Ashley, a mom of seven children. She set a goal that seemed almost impossible, but it gave her the motivation to put forth super effort to make it happen. She needed to feel like she was shooting for the stars. And dreaming big led her to achieving big dreams.

In January 2012, I decided that I was finally going to create a successful business by the end of the year. I had tried and failed so many times before, but I was determined this year to keep throwing spaghetti against the wall until something finally stuck.

I set an income goal to match my husband's, not because I felt like it was a reachable goal, but because I wanted to aim high. Earning enough to get my nails done and buying a few new shirts each month didn't excite and invigorate me. I wanted a goal that seemed impossible so that when I did hit it, I'd feel like Superwoman.

I stumbled across a short motivational speech on YouTube by Art Williams entitled "Just Do It." Watching this talk became part of my morning ritual that revved me up and honed in my focus to accomplish all the tasks that I didn't necessarily love completing, but that were contributing to the bottom line of my business.

I worked most days on my business and focused primarily on tasks that would bring me closer to my goal. If a particular income stream wasn't paying off, I cut it. If I had a new idea, I jumped in and tried it. The method for meeting my goal was not important to me; the actual achievement of the goal was my top priority.

I'm happy to report that I did meet the goal that I set in October 2012. Even more exciting than meeting the goal, I doubled my income in November and then tripled it in December!

After blowing my original goal out of the water, I asked myself, what was different this time? Why did I finally succeed? I realized that every year prior, my goal was attainable. I was setting small, uninspiring goals that didn't require massive action. For me personally, if it doesn't required massive action, I generally decide that it's not worth doing.

If I'm presented with going for the impossible or going for average, I'll strive for the impossible every time. If you are motivated to succeed when someone tells you that you can't, give it a shot. Set a goal that would completely change your life forever, and then work every day to make it happen.

IT TAKES DISCIPLINE

Setting small goals and having a positive attitude will help propel you toward goal-setting success. However, if you do those things, but you don't have the discipline to follow through with your goals, you won't get very far.

You are only guaranteed success if you have the discipline, perseverance, and commitment to follow through with your goals. More on that in the next chapter!

GET PRACTICAL

1. What are your current goals? Brainstorm and come up with a list of one to three goals you want to focus on right now.

2. If you've chosen larger goals, be sure to break these down into bite-size pieces, and create a plan of action for the next six months. It's much easier to follow through with goals when

you've broken them down into small, doable pieces.

3. Once you've determined your goals, write them down, and stick them in a very conspicuous location (like in the fridge, on your bathroom mirror, or as the home screen on your phone).

4. Set up a weekly appointment with yourself to review and reevaluate your goals and how things are going. If possible, also find someone to regularly keep you accountable to stick with your goals.

4

Discipline Is Not a Bad Word

Discipline is the bridge between goals and accomplishment.
—JIM ROHN

Goal: Experience significant lifelong change through cultivating small, daily habits.

Strategy: Choose one habit that will make a big impact, and implement it consistently for three to six weeks until it becomes something you do without thinking. Then move on to the next habit.

I was born into a very athletic family. My dad ran track in high school and college, winning many awards. Years have passed, but he still runs a few miles almost every morning. My mom rarely misses a day of exercise—either a brisk walk or bike ride of a few miles, or both.

As a result, when I was growing up, exercise was something my parents highly emphasized. We did a variety of different exercise programs over the years—including going through the entire Royal Canadian Air Force exercise program. (Yes, my mom could be a bit of a drill sergeant!)

For one of our exercise programs, she tested our running endurance by seeing how long it took us to run a mile. She decided to have us start at the corner of one country road where we lived and run to the one-mile marker while she timed us.

For my other athletic siblings, this was a piece of cake. Me? Not so much. In fact, I made it about two-thirds of a mile when my body completely gave out. I couldn't take another step, and I collapsed in the middle of the road and just lay there catching my breath for a few minutes.

To this day, my family still laughs about my middle-of-the-road breakdown. While I laugh heartily with them (because it was pretty comical!), for years it solidified my belief that I wasn't a runner. So I never even bothered to try running and instead got my regular exercise by working out on an elliptical, biking, walking, or doing exercise DVDs.

A few years ago, I stumbled upon Tony Horton's P90X program from a link online. After watching the videos and reading more about it, I decided to take the plunge, buy it, and follow through with the ninety-day program. While I might not be as athletic as the rest of my family, I am stubborn. And it's a good thing, because I needed every ounce of determination I could muster to stick with the strenuous P90X workout program.

At first, I could barely pull off seven to eight push-ups at a time. But as I stuck with it and practiced and practiced and practiced, I was amazed at how my strength increased. Pretty soon, I could drop and do twenty push-ups no sweat.

After ninety days, not only had I developed a lot of muscles, but I'd also significantly increased my personal resolve. So I decided to go out on a limb and try running again. To my surprise, I knocked out over a mile without feeling winded!

This kicked my motivation into high gear, and I resolved to become a runner. I started the Couch to 5K program, and little bit by little bit, my running stamina improved. There were many days when I felt like I was going to throw up or pass out on the treadmill as I increased my time and my distance, but I didn't give up. And, after many months of practice, I ran my first 5K race. I'm now training for a 10K with my sights set on eventually going for a half marathon.

There was no way I could run a 5K on day one or even day twenty-one. It took months of disciplining myself to get up, get on my running shoes, and get on the treadmill. Day in, day out. Whether I felt like it or not. All of that work was every bit worth it when I crossed the finish line at the 5K race. My daily discipline had paid off, and little bit by little bit, I had become something I never thought I could be: I was a runner!

> The only discipline that lasts is self-discipline.
> —BUM PHILLIPS

DISCIPLINE STARTS FROM WITHIN

Many of us long to be more disciplined. We crave order and peace. We want to be better managers of our time and lives. We want to follow through with our good intentions.

So we buy the best-selling book that promises to help stop procrastinating and get things done. We listen to podcasts that offer three ways to develop more self-control. We download a printable, household-organization planner and think it will magically whip our houses into shape. We take a workshop and hope it will motivate us to become more disciplined. We pray. We wish. We dream.

Fancy systems or a three-step program won't turn you into a super disciplined person. Change must come from within. You have to believe you can change. You have to want to change. And you need to have something worth changing for, like an inspiring, audacious goal. The bottom line is: if you're not willing to put forth effort, you're never going to get very far in life.

YOU WERE MADE FOR MORE THAN THE STATUS QUO

I'm not going to paint a roses-and-rainbows picture of self-discipline for you. Because it's not always fun. Or glamorous. Or easy. It requires swimming upstream, going against the tide, and doing hard things. But it does pay off.

I don't watch a lot of TV, except when the Olympics are on. Then I'm pretty well glued to the screen for two weeks. I find the Olympic Games and the stories of the participants so inspiring.

Think about those athletes. Did they get where they are just by showing up to a few practices? Or working out for only a few minutes a few times a week? No, they have endured years of daily practice—getting up early, training, improving their strength and agility, and fueling their bodies with the right nutrients.

No athlete makes it to the Olympics without exerting enormous amounts of self-discipline—probably more than most of us can fathom. They push themselves through pain, injury, exhaustion, and fatigue. They don't give up when the going gets tough, monotonous, or boring. Even if they tire of doing the same thing day after day after day, they continue to do it. Winners aren't quitters.

> We are what we repeatedly do, excellence then is not an act, but a habit.
> —ARISTOTLE

While most of us probably will never compete in the Olympics, if you want to live on purpose, you'll have to have the mind-set of an Olympian. You'll have to make sacrifices. Get up earlier. Give up late-night dinners. Drive an older model car. Say no to that piece of chocolate cake. Study instead of seeing that movie. Invest time in your family instead of filling your social calendar with parties. That's okay. In the long run, those sacrifices and your countercultural living choices will pay off with big dividends.

If you're willing to put forth the effort, you are going to reap the benefits. You might not win an Olympic gold medal, but you'll win big in other areas. I promise.

EXPECTING BIG RESULTS FAST

We live in a culture that expects instant results. Consequently, there is a disdain for delayed gratification and a lack of respect for the self-discipline required to achieve difficult goals. People fail because they don't stick with something for long enough.

Before my husband and I got married, we sat down and did

a lot of calculating to see how little money we could survive on. Our goal was to make it through Jesse's six remaining months of undergraduate school and the following three years of law school without going into debt.

We had the money saved up and set aside to pay for school, but we didn't have much else. We figured that if we both worked part-time, we could make close to $1,000 per month. Considering that our rent was over half of that amount, we had around $125 a week left over to cover utilities, transportation, food, and other living expenses. When you add all that up, $125 is more like pocket change. Still, we were determined to make it work. It meant shopping at the thrift store, clipping coupons and looking for the best bargains, driving a used vehicle, packing sack lunches and skipping dinners out, and living in a small basement apartment.

We were able to press forward because we knew the future rewards we would reap from our efforts. We would have financial freedom. We wouldn't be chained to law school loans. Without debt, we would be in a better position to reach our long-term goals of owning a home and other real estate debt-free. Most importantly, we would be in a position to give generously to those in need. Keeping those long-term benefits in mind helped us get through the temporary discomforts.

It wasn't easy to make those sacrifices. Both of us had moments when we wanted to give in. I remember one time when several of our acquaintances from law school were getting together for a party. We really wanted to go, but they had asked that everyone chip in four dollars per person to cover the expenses. There was no way we could afford to pay eight dollars for both of us to go to the party, and I was really embarrassed to ask if I could bring food instead (that I'd gotten free with coupons!). When I sent that e-mail to the party hostess, I wanted to cry because money was so tight for us. (By the way, the hostess graciously e-mailed back and said she'd love for us to bring food—and we had a great time, despite my initial embarrassment.)

There were many more moments like that when I felt discouraged and worn down as I considered our lean budget. But we kept plodding on, constantly reminding ourselves that someday it would be worth it to be debt-free.

And it has been every bit worth it.

Today we still adhere to a strict written budget. We have more breathing room in our budget than during law school, and we mutually decided to allow "splurges" every now and then (like our dinner at the Cheesecake Factory last Friday night). We still do our best to keep our expenses and expenditures to a minimum. This enables us to live on much less than we make so we can invest our money for the future and give to others who are in need. None of this would be possible if we hadn't made many, many sacrifices during those first few years of our marriage.

> Discipline is remembering what you want.
> —DAVID CAMPBELL

HOW BADLY DO YOU WANT IT?

What are some of your goals? Habits you want to change? Things you hope to accomplish in one, five, or ten years from now? Where do you want to be financially? What do you hope to achieve in your career? Your health? Your family?

Do you want to go to graduate school? Do you want to lose twenty pounds? Do you want to get out of debt? Do you want to get a handle on organizing your house? Do you want to build a work-from-home business? Do you want to consistently get up early each morning to get a head start on the rest of the day?

You may want to simply start enjoying your life and living on purpose instead of running ragged, feeling lost without any direction, and struggling to find meaning in the middle of busy and crazy schedules.

WHEN THERE'S A WILL, THERE'S USUALLY A WAY

Whatever your goals are, you won't be able to reach them without making some sacrifices, especially in the short term. You can't change whatever situation you're in unless you also change the way you're doing something.

You have to be willing to cut back, give up things, spend your time differently, and say no more often. You may even risk hearing negative comments from others. How willing you are to make changes is directly dependent upon how motivated you are to get where you want to go.

I've found that if I want something badly enough, I can usually find a way to make it work. It won't always be easy, fun, or glamorous to make short-term sacrifices, but it will be worth it.

SHORT-TERM SACRIFICES FOR LONG-TERM BENEFITS

What simple, short-term sacrifices can you make to help you get to where you want to be or achieve what you hope to accomplish? One of the ways we saved money when times were particularly tight was by owning just one vehicle. Since I worked from home, this was more feasible than it would be for some families. But it was still a sacrifice. It meant that I was homebound pretty much all day, every day except for evenings and weekends. I learned to love being home. My children and I could still walk to nearby places. And we invited lots of friends over to our house, since we didn't have a car to drive to theirs. To this day, I still look back fondly on those years when life was so simple.

SIGN ME UP! WHERE DO I START?

As I've said, there is no magic formula that will automatically transform you into a disciplined person. It takes time. And consistency. And not giving up. Here are some ideas to help you get to that place of self-discipline.

Start Small

You'll never get anywhere if you don't take the first step. It's fun to dream big dreams and make big plans, but executing them happens one small step at a time.

Take blogging, for instance. It seems these days that almost everyone has a blog. Some people have one hoping to make money from it; others want to share their thoughts, experience, or insights. It's not that hard to create a blog and write a few posts. But maintaining a successful blog—whether that's defined by the number of subscribers, the income it generates, or something entirely different—is the result of massive amounts of effort, determination, consistency, and perseverance.

This is not an easy thing to do, and it's why so many bloggers give up after a few months. Unless you're already a celebrity, there's no such thing as overnight blogging success. It takes hard work, sweat, and more hard work. It may be a few months before you ever see any results from the hours of labor invested into your blog. But if you stick with it, your efforts will pay off.

Faithfulness in the little things will eventually add up to big progress. This principle works across the board. If you want to start a business, start it on the side while still employed at your full-time job. Work evenings, Saturdays, or whenever you can fit it in. Grow only when you're able to afford it and have more time. Looking to declutter your home? Start by working on one room a week. Or take a few weeks and tackle your downstairs floor. Then move upstairs.

If you want to get on a written budget, the thought of going from no budget at all to a to-the-penny, written budget can be overwhelming. Start by committing to a grocery budget for the next three months. The lessons you'll learn through implementing and following a grocery budget will likely carry over to many other aspects of your finances. And the momentum you achieve from being disciplined will propel and inspire you to success in other areas.

Don't let the thought of working out four times a week for the next six months overwhelm you. Don't let the seeming impossibility for you to limit or eliminate your Facebook or TV time stress you out. Don't let the thought of saving for your children's college fund make you want to give up. Instead of looking at your goal as a whole, focus on one small thing you can do today, this week, or this month to make some headway. I promise you won't feel so defeated!

Remember, big progress begins with small changes. It's easy to want to overhaul your life overnight, but if you want to see success throughout the long term, do yourself a favor and start with little steps.

Small steps might seem minuscule and microscopic. You might feel as though you're hardly getting anywhere. But keep going. Don't give up. Press forward. When you do, I promise you'll start to reap the fruits of your efforts. Someday soon you'll look back and realize that all of those tiny, seemingly insignificant changes added up to greater success than you ever dreamed was possible.

> The best time to plant a tree is twenty years ago. The second best time is today.
> —AFRICAN PROVERB

Get Focused

Without discipline in my lifestyle, I am apt to feel frustrated for wasting time. When I get distracted, procrastinate, or choose to do what I want to do over what I should do (e.g., surf the web versus writing an article that is due), I usually end up stressed too, because it results in me being behind schedule or late to an event.

If you are struggling to stay focused, step back and examine if there are things that are serving as major distractions. Are you on Facebook or reading blogs instead of going to bed early so you can get up early? Set up LeechBlock on your computer so you can't get on Facebook during the workday or on certain blogs after dinner.[1]

Are you giving in to the temptation to eat two brownies

every night, even though you're trying to lose five pounds? Get rid of the brownies and don't make them anymore. Seriously, it's better to throw them in the trash if they are keeping you from sticking with your goals.

Do you always answer your phone while in the middle of a work project, a house chore, the quality time with your kids, or a workout? It's great to be social and connected with others, but if a call is not urgent, there is no need to stop what you're doing to answer it.

WHAT YOU WANT TO KNOW

Q: Do you think that multitasking is unproductive?

A: I'm a big believer in focused intensity when it comes to many projects. If you want to get anything worthwhile done in life, you've got to have focus. And I like to take that one step further and make it focused intensity.

WHAT IS FOCUSED INTENSITY?

Focused intensity is zeroing in on one specific project and giving it your entire concentration and energy for a determined length of time. I like to set a time limit on it and then challenge myself to see how much I can get done in that time frame.

For instance, if I'm working on writing a blog post, an article, or a chapter in my next book, I'll usually shut everything down on my computer, shut my office door, set the timer for ten or fifteen minutes, and work as hard as I can until the timer goes off.

When I work with this kind of focused intensity, I can get a lot done in a short amount of time. Whereas, if I'm scattered all over the place—trying to write a post while checking and answering e-mails, keeping up with what's going on my Facebook page, and refreshing my blog comments page—it will take me a very long time to get any writing done, and I probably won't do a quality job of it.

WHEN SHOULD YOU WORK WITH FOCUSED INTENSITY?

Everyone is different, but I've found that I cannot write well when there are a dozen distractions going on at once. I also find that I'm not able to think and process ideas and post outlines well if I'm constantly interrupted.

I've found it typically takes me three to five times longer to finish a post or writing project when I'm constantly interrupted than it does when I can work with focused intensity. So writing is one area where I always choose times of day when I know I can work with minimal interruptions (during the early morning hours, during afternoon quiet times, or on Saturdays).

ARE THERE TIMES WHEN IT'S GOOD TO MULTITASK?

There are many, many other things I do that don't require the same level of focus that writing does. And I'm all about multitasking if the end result means greater productivity.

I read while I do my walking warm-up and cool-down

on the treadmill. I knit while I'm watching a movie with the family. I scrub my kitchen floor while I talk on the phone. Or I put bread in the bread machine to mix while I'm chatting with a friend who is over.

There's no point in doing one thing when you can just as easily do two things well. I intentionally plan ahead for these opportunities—often even writing them on my daily to-do list. If I know I'm going to be heading to an appointment, I'll make a note to bring a certain book or writing project, depending upon the appointment. If I know that we're going to be having a family movie night or I'm having a friend over, I'll make a note to make sure and get out my knitting or other handwork project.

By planning ahead like this, I'm able to use the time more productively, and in turn, I'm able to chip away at my weekly goal list—all while multitasking. So before I know it, projects are getting done without me putting a whole lot of extra effort into them.

That said, make sure when you are multitasking that you are actually being more productive. Sometimes, in trying to multitask, you end up getting less done and making a mess of multiple things.

Do the Hardest Things First

Mark Twain wisely said, "If you eat a frog first thing in the morning that will probably be the worst thing you do all day." Brian Tracy wrote an entire book based upon this quote titled

Eat That Frog! 21 Great Ways to Stop Procrastinating and Get More Done in Less Time.[2]

Tracy suggests that if you start your day by doing the things you like least first, you'll get them out of the way so you can enjoy your day more and be more productive and fulfilled. This might mean exercising, tidying the house, or doing laundry right after you wake up.

Challenged by this idea, I started applying it to my laundry pile. Instead of letting it sit and grow to an overwhelming size, I start a load of laundry first thing in the morning, switch it to the dryer before breakfast, and then fold it mid-morning. While I haven't been successful at doing this every day, on the days that I have done this, I've been amazed at how well it works. (Why has it taken me years of running my own home to figure out this principle?)

When I do one load a day, I'm able to stay on top of the laundry. The dirty laundry piles never get out of control, and it takes no more than fifteen minutes a day for upkeep. It's a simple yet eye-opening illustration of how getting the most dreaded tasks out of the way right off the bat gives me so much momentum for the rest of the day.

Now, I have to tell you that I'm still very much a work in progress when it comes to procrastination. In fact, just last night I suffered the consequences of putting something off. An article deadline crept up on me seemingly out of nowhere. All of a sudden I realized I only had four days until it was going to be posted on a particular blog. *No worries,* I thought. *I'll have plenty of time on Saturday.* After all, it was only Friday, and my deadline wasn't until Tuesday.

But then on Friday night I came down with a really bad case

of the flu. Saturday and Sunday I could barely open my eyes, let alone think about trying to write an article. By Monday, I was still feeling sick, but I was well enough to sit up in bed and try to catch up on business work and e-mails. Since I was behind and somewhat in a daze due to the fever, all of a sudden it was 9 p.m. and my article wasn't done. So what did I do, even though I really should have been sleeping? Yes, I stayed up and finished writing that article so that it could be posted at 6 a.m. as scheduled.

This experience was a great reminder of why procrastination is such a bad idea. I should never wait until the last minute or tell myself, "I've got plenty of time" and then put something off. Because you never know what tomorrow might bring. I encourage you to get your hardest tasks done early so you can relax and enjoy the fruit and fulfillment of not procrastinating.

> I have committed to setting weekly goals and getting up earlier each morning. If I don't feel motivated to do them, I remember all the benefits that will come from staying focused. In particular, achieving these two goals gives me more time to spend with my young children and makes me feel less rushed. Remembering these things helps me to stay on track.
> —JACKIE

Stop Making Excuses

I've had a lifelong struggle with getting places on time. For years, I always came up with an excuse for my tardiness—I was stuck waiting for a train to pass, the traffic was bad, I couldn't find a parking spot. You name the excuse, I've probably used it. And while many of these excuses were legitimate, they are also inevitabilities that come with the territory of driving . . . things I should know by now to plan ahead for.

So in reality, it wasn't that the traffic was crazy or that the parking lot was packed; it was that I wasn't disciplined enough to plan ahead and leave on time. If I stop waiting until the last minute to get out the door and allow an extra fifteen- to thirty-minute margin just in case, I'm able to get places on time—or occasionally even a little early! It's still a struggle, but slowly (ever so slowly), I'm making progress in this area. And it all started when I stopped making excuses for my lack of discipline.

Excuses never get you anywhere. Instead of sitting and making excuses, invest the time and effort it takes to make excuses, and consider how you can set yourself up for success in achieving your goals. For instance, if you're trying to get up earlier each day but you find that you always fall back to sleep or hit the Snooze button, don't just give up and make the excuse, "I'm not a morning person." Maybe you're not, but until you've at least tried getting up early for four to six weeks, you can't make that claim.

Celebrate Milestones

I'm all about changing habits, setting goals, and working hard toward accomplishing them. I also believe in celebrating milestones along the way. If you hit a goal, set up a reward system to treat yourself. After you achieve a savings goal, allot yourself a small, reasonable amount of money to "splurge" on something. If you lose a certain amount of weight this month, get a pedicure. If your house is finally organized and clutter-free, go out to dinner at your favorite restaurant. Just don't celebrate by doing something that will sabotage your efforts, like binge-ing at McDonald's after you lost ten pounds!

My reward for accomplishing my tasks is often relaxing with a good book for thirty minutes at the end of the day or watching a movie with my husband. For some of you, those rewards might not sound exciting, but they are both things I love to do. And I can enjoy them even more when I know that my tasks are accomplished!

If you need an extra motivator on a daily basis, you can reward yourself after "eating a frog" first thing in the morning. When you've accomplished your most dreaded task for the day, do something nice for yourself. Enjoy a piece of dark chocolate, savor a cup of coffee, or take a bubble bath. A reward will give you something to look forward to when you're in the midst of doing your hard tasks. It will also give you motivation to accomplish them more quickly.

A DISCIPLINE BONUS

One of the most amazing things I've learned in this journey is that discipline begets discipline. When I am disciplined in one area, that resolve spills over into other areas.

The early-bird principle, for instance, has set so many other good habits in motion. I have more time to pray and study the Bible. I have more time to exercise. I have more time to get a head start on the day before my kids wake up. Intentionally making one consistent habit change can slowly lead to amazing transformation in many areas of your life.

Charles Duhigg agrees with me in his book *The Power of Habit*.[3] He challenges you to focus their efforts on those habits that are going to give you the biggest bang for your buck. That is, zero in your efforts and energies on purposeful changes that are going to spill over into other areas of your life. He calls these "keystone habits," and here's what he wrote about them in a blog post on LifeHacker:

> Some habits, say researchers, are more important than others because they have the power to start a chain reaction, shifting other patterns as they move through our lives. Keystone habits influence how we work, eat, play, live, spend, and communicate. Keystone habits start a process that, over time, transforms everything.
>
> This, then, is the answer of where to start: focus on keystone habits, those patterns that, when they start to shift, dislodge and remake other habits.[4]

So find those "keystone habits," pick one to focus on developing for the next three to six weeks, don't give up, and keep with it even when you don't feel like it. One day soon, you may wake up and realize you've changed your whole life . . . just by beginning with one simple habit!

GET PRACTICAL

What are some areas in your life where you lack self-discipline? It could be your health. Maybe you are eating more junk food than nutritious snacks or not getting enough exercise. Maybe you repeatedly hit the Snooze button every morning or waste a lot of time watching TV. Think about how not having discipline in these areas affects your life. Are you still carrying around twenty extra pounds? Do you feel sluggish every day? Do you not have enough time for anything? Do you lack focus in planning or carrying out your day intentionally? If you focused on changing your habits, how would your life change?

In the next twenty-four hours, find fifteen minutes to sit down and make a list of all the good habits you want to develop in your life and the bad habits you want to reverse. This is not an exercise to overwhelm you; it's an exercise to get it all written down on paper so it's not sitting in your brain nagging you.

Once you've made an exhaustive list, prioritize the top three habits that would make the most difference were you to implement them tomorrow. Then take a deep breath and set your paper aside in a safe place.

Start working on one habit at a time for the next twenty-one days. When you feel like the current habit you're working on has truly become a habit, then you can start on the second habit. Once you've mastered the third habit, pull out your exhaustive list and start making the next thing a priority. Remember to take it slowly—even if you're tempted to accelerate to the next habit.

5

Be Intentional with Your Bank Account

> The highest use of capital is not to make more money but to make money do more for the betterment of life.
>
> —HENRY FORD

Goal: Get your finances in order so you can spend, save, and give with purpose.

Strategy: Develop short-term and long-term financial goals and then create a plan to carry those goals out.

I well remember sitting on the floor in the living room of our rental home in Kansas City. I wept as I held our second child, a baby girl. Between heaving sobs, I lashed out at my husband. I threw at him all the feelings of frustration and hopelessness that had boiled up inside.

Jesse didn't deserve to be berated. It wasn't his fault that the job market was bad and that no one was hiring. He was trying wholeheartedly to find a job. But our bank account was quickly dwindling. And I was scared.

Was he ever going to find a job? How were we going to pay for the rent and utilities? Was he really trying hard enough to find work? I cried. I ranted. I even threatened to leave. Looking back, I realize I was acting overly dramatic, but at the time I was dead serious.

My husband and I are blessed to come from families who recognized the importance of making wise financial decisions. When we got engaged in 2002, the year before Jesse planned to enter law school, we discussed and prayed about finances. Both of us were debt-free and committed to living beneath our means. However, in crunching the numbers, we knew it would take some extreme creativity and frugality to stay out of debt through law school. We were determined but had no idea how hard the road would be.

We got married in January 2003, right before Jesse's last semester of college, and we practiced frugality from the get-go. We honeymooned in an inexpensive hotel in a neighboring state, brought our own food, shopped at the dollar store to supplement, and only splurged once to eat out at Subway. Back from our honeymoon, we rented the cheapest apartment we could find and outfitted it with furniture hand-me-downs from friends and family, plus a used couch. We both worked as many hours as we could at our part-time jobs and saved every penny possible. We learned that a strong marriage is not built on how much money you have, but on the depth of your love and commitment to one another.

During Jesse's first year of law school, we worked hard to make ends meet. I worked part-time for three different families as a nanny, plus had a regular babysitting gig. Jesse telecommuted part-time for his dad's business. Between our incomes, we barely made enough to cover all our expenses. We needed a more stable, long-term source of income, and I didn't want to be working so many jobs, so in my spare time, I started researching work-from-home jobs.

> Sacrifice is a part of life. It's supposed to be. It's not something to regret. It's something to aspire to.
> —MITCH ALBOM

In 2004, soon after Jesse began his second semester of law school, we found out we were expecting. I was so sick during the pregnancy that I had to quit working. This cut our income by more than half and created quite a bit of anxiety. But it also gave me more incentive to look into creative ways to make money from home. I spent most of my days in bed with the laptop researching possibilities and experimenting with different ideas. Though I made many, many mistakes in the process (more on that in a little while), much of what I learned during those months laid the foundation for what would later become MoneySavingMom.com.

KNOW WHERE YOU'RE GOING

So many people dream of getting out of debt, paying cash for another vehicle, paying off their houses early, or giving more generously to others. Very few people, however, get beyond the dreaming stage. Instead, they drive around and around without a map, wishing they could go somewhere without ever determining where they want to go.

If you don't know where you are going, you'll never reach your destination. You have to set financial goals that are right for your family. Every family is in a different situation with different needs, different circumstances, and different short-term and long-term goals. For us, one of our first financial goals was to stay out of debt during law school. We couldn't think or plan much beyond that because we had to make it through the three years of law school first. That was enough to focus on at that time.

If you're married, you need to sit down with your spouse and develop these financial goals together. If you're not on the same page in your marriage, it's going to be hard to make much progress on your financial goals.

To determine your goals, ask yourselves: Where do we want to be financially a year from now? Five years from now? Ten?

Brainstorm answers. Your ideas may include getting out of credit card debt, paying off medical bills, paying off your vehicles, buying a new car, saving for your kids' college fund, saving up for retirement, or putting aside money for a family vacation. Maybe right now you need to focus on staying out of debt—like we did while Jesse was in law school.

After the brainstorming session, look at your list of ideas and pick two or three to adopt as your financial goals. I recommend choosing one goal you think could be fairly easily accomplished in the next six months, one in the next year or two, and one that seems quite audacious (but doable with diligence, hard work, and commitment) with a five-year or more end date. Also, be sure you use the SMART principles (see chapter 3) when creating your goals.

Here are five examples of goals I recommend that you make your top priority (in this order), based upon recommendations you'll find in Dave Ramsey's book *The Total Money Makeover*[1]:

- Set up a small emergency fund of at least one month's expenses (in case the unexpected happens, like a death in the family or a job loss).
- Pay off your credit cards and any outstanding medical debt.
- Increase your emergency fund to cover three to six months' worth of expenses.
- Save to pay cash for your next large purchase (like a car).
- Save up to put a large down payment on a house, or aggressively work on paying off your current mortgage.

Once you determine your top two or three goals, write them down and post them where you'll see them every day—maybe right next to where you posted your other goals you came up with in chapter 3.

Now, just like you did earlier, start breaking them down into bite-size chunks. For example, if you want to lower your credit card debt, you might consider setting aside two hundred dollars each month to go directly toward paying down your debt. If you want to beef up your savings, aim to save 10 percent of each paycheck.

No more pie-in-the-sky financial dreams. Now you have concrete goals to serve as the driving force for decisions your family makes.

FINANCIAL AWAKENINGS

I mentioned Dave Ramsey above, and I can't recommend his radio show, events, or books enough. He's a well-known financial expert who gives empowering and biblically based financial advice to help people get out of debt. During the last year of law school, Jesse discovered his radio show and kept coming to me all pumped about what he was learning.

I wasn't too excited. After all, I stubbornly thought, weren't we pretty smart when it came to finances? Did we really need some guru with a radio show telling us what to do? I mean, c'mon, we were debt-free, we were living on a budget, we were living beneath our means, and we were giving—even on a very small income. What more could some guy on the radio teach us about money?

But Jesse persisted in encouraging me to give this expert a chance. I finally gave in and begrudgingly agreed to go with my husband through Dave's thirteen-week financial program, Financial Peace University.[2]

I was hooked after the first class. Dave taught me things like the pros and cons of different kinds of insurance, what mutual funds are, and how to prepare for retirement—and he did it all in an engaging and understandable way. Not only that, but going through Financial Peace University also caused me to have a complete paradigm shift in my thinking about money. Truth be told, I'd never really thought long term about financial goals. Our one goal was to stay out of debt and make it through law school. Beyond that, I didn't have anything long range that I was shooting for.

Dave Ramsey gave us a vision. He inspired us to think big,

plan ahead, and dream big dreams. Most of all, we were motivated to get our family in the best financial shape possible so that we could bless and help others by being generous givers. We finally began to learn what it meant to be intentional in how we handled money.

When Jesse and I were finished with Financial Peace University, we sat down and made some big goals (like the seemingly impossible one of buying a house with cash within five years of Jesse finishing law school). At the time, our goals were ambitious and some even far-fetched, but we decided to aim for the stars. We figured even if we didn't hit them, we'd likely make more traction than if we hadn't aimed at all!

PASSING ON GOOD FINANCIAL HABITS TO OUR CHILDREN

It's important to pass on wisdom to your kids, especially as it concerns money. Here are three ways to instill in them a sound financial mind-set:

- Model financial stewardship. Children learn more by example than through our words.
- Introduce financial talk from the beginning. We started talking about debt, mortgages, credit cards, budgets, and giving with our children when they were only toddlers. Explain basic financial concepts in language they'll understand.
- Give your children opportunities to earn, spend, and save. We have paid chores and unpaid chores at our house. Unpaid chores are those chores our children do because they're members of our household (such as

making their beds, cleaning their rooms, vacuuming, helping with the dishes, etc.). The paid chores are extra ones that our children can choose to do if they want to earn some extra money (such as cleaning the car or cleaning Mom and Dad's bathroom).

A TIPPING POINT

When Jesse finished law school in 2006, by the grace of God we had no debt and a few thousand dollars in savings. Jesse passed the bar and got a great job. We were elated! For the first time since we were married, Jesse was making a good full-time income, and we finally felt like we had some financial stability.

Soon we were thrilled to find out we were expecting our second child. We started looking at the possibility of moving from our little basement apartment to a duplex. And we even began thinking of how fun it was going to be to be able to afford to splurge on little things every now and then.

But our elation was soon deflated as that great job Jesse had didn't last long, and he was left looking for another position—something that was hard to come by with little experience and a tight job market. After many weeks of searching and praying, Jesse was offered a new position, albeit one he wasn't thrilled about. But it was a job; it would pay the bills. And that's what mattered most at that point. So we packed up and moved.

Jesse started his new job with high hopes. But within the first month, Jesse realized his new position was a lot harder than he had anticipated. The learning curve was steep, the hours were long, the work was stressful, and the office environment was tense.

PRESSURE STARTS TO BUILD

The job we had thought was a blessing began to wear on Jesse. He was almost always exhausted and stressed. He was given more big projects, which meant even longer hours. Easygoing and fun-loving Jesse was so overloaded at work that he rarely smiled or enjoyed life anymore. I tried to encourage him as best as I knew how, but the pressure he was dealing with at work was enormous.

The stress trickled down to me, and I began neglecting my own health. Soon I started experiencing issues in my pregnancy. I became severely anemic and ended up in the hospital for five days in my thirty-fourth week. My midwife and doctor were worried I was going to have to be induced early since my hemoglobin and platelet counts were so low. But God intervened, and I was able to carry Kaitlynn to thirty-eight weeks before being induced.

My health issues were a wake-up call to both of us. We finally admitted something major needed to happen in Jesse's job situation, or he needed to quit. The thought of quitting was scary. It meant having no insurance and, of course, a loss of income. We felt trapped, but we prayed and thought about the situation long and hard.

More and more it felt like it was the right thing for Jesse to resign. But what about our financial goals and hopes and dreams? Were we defeating ourselves by cutting off most of our income? How would we survive if Jesse wasn't able to get a new job right away? We only had enough in savings to live on for a few months. And my income from my online business was certainly not enough for us to survive on at that point.

Unexpectedly, Jesse was asked to resign. While this came as a shock, we took it as God's clear direction for us. But we didn't know what the next step might be, or how we were going to live if Jesse didn't find a job quickly. So we were left without our primary income source in a new city with little support, few friends, and even fewer business contacts.

At first, we were pretty confident Jesse could find work that would at least pay the bills. How hard could it be? Apparently, a lot harder than we thought. Days turned into weeks, and weeks turned into months.

Jesse applied for every job he was remotely qualified for. We prayed harder than we'd ever prayed. We contacted anyone and everyone who might have a possible job lead. We followed up with every application. But no one was calling to offer Jesse an interview, let alone a job.

That's when our marriage hit a hard place. I wish I could say that I kept a cheerful attitude through all of this. On the contrary, I woke up every morning with a sick feeling in the pit of my stomach wondering how much more we could take. Though I'm ashamed to admit it, I felt so alone, scared, and stressed that I often became angry with my husband.

Thankfully, because we didn't have any debt and were still living on a strict budget, the job loss didn't plunge us into complete financial ruin. I can't even fathom what it would have been like had we piled up debt in law school or bought a house and lived more extravagantly after law school. The added financial strains may have further deteriorated or even destroyed our relationship.

WHAT YOU WANT TO KNOW ▮▮▮▮▮▮▮▮▮▮▮▮▮▮▮▮

Q: My husband recently got laid off, and we have to live on my income. I am now in charge of our budget. While I'm diligent in paying our bills on time and watching our spending habits so we stay afloat, he doesn't seem to care as much. With our different views and attitudes about money, how can we work together to get on the same page?

A: I'm not a marriage counselor. I can only speak from my personal experience as to what has worked for my husband and me in our ten years of marriage. My advice may or may not work in your situation, so you may want to consider seeking professional counsel.

First, accept that you are different. You didn't marry your clone, which is probably a good thing! We all need someone a little different to help balance us out. Instead of being discouraged or disheartened that your husband has different opinions, accept him as he is. Don't try to change him or make him just like you; it won't work. Believe me, I've tried.

Second, learn to appreciate the differences. I tend to be ultrafrugal, while my husband tends to be more extravagant (at least according to my standards). This can be a source of frustration for both of us, but we've also learned to appreciate these differences and learn from each other. Together, we make a much stronger, more balanced team than either of us would be on our own. That's the beauty of learning to appreciate and build on differences instead of letting them get in the way of resolution.

Third, communicate openly. My husband does all the bill paying and budget tallying because he enjoys that sort of thing, while I find it tedious. But we work together on creating and maintaining our budget. I heartily encourage all couples to have regularly scheduled monthly budget accountability meetings to discuss your financial situation, create and revise your written budget, talk about financial issues that have come up, and review your financial goals. If you've never done this sort of thing before, it may be difficult or uncomfortable at first, but I promise it's ultimately worth it.

There is one rule that must be followed at these meetings: they must include mutual discussions. Don't try to force anything on your spouse. There should be give and take and open talk. You must both be willing to compromise and talk things through to come to a point of agreement.

Dragging your spouse to the meeting and berating him for his handling of money won't get you anywhere except in the wrong direction. However, graciously explaining to your spouse how you've been struggling with the financial situation and feeling like there is constant tension in your life as a result of not being on the same page will probably get you somewhere. And showing that you are open to compromising and reaching an agreement that is mutually beneficial will go a long way too.

KEEP ON KEEPING ON

While our marriage was in bad shape, we did make one good decision—to be as creative and resourceful as we could to avoid accessing our emergency fund (an account where we had saved up almost three months' worth of expenses). The idea for MoneySavingMom.com was born during this time. I'd learned a lot about blogging and monetizing a blog over the past few years. I'd written quite a bit on supermarket savings on the site I had, and these articles had been popular. People were constantly asking me for practical money-saving advice, so I figured starting a frugal, money-saving blog might work well. Jesse was excited about this new venture, and we launched the site in the fall of 2007.

While it seemed like we were getting nowhere in the job search, God was doing some amazing things behind the scenes. In fact, our lives were about to be turned upside down—in a wonderful way!

With the downturn of the economy, MoneySavingMom.com took off with a bang. In fact, within three months, the site was getting twelve to fifteen thousand page views every day. And it kept growing! After a year (and countless hours of work and experimenting), MoneySavingMom.com began to bring in a steady full-time income.

It was one of those instances of being in the right place at the right time, persevering, and God wildly blessing a project. I'd started the blog hoping it would someday provide a steady source of side income for our family. I never could have imagined that six years later, it would be one of the highest trafficked personal finance blogs on the web, read by more than a million people each month! And that side income I'd hoped for? Well, that goal got blown out of the water as it provides more than a full-time income for our family, pays the salaries of all my team members, and allows us to give generously to needs in our community and around the world. The whole thing still amazes me!

I wasn't the only one reaping the rewards from years of hard work and struggle. In October 2008, we moved back home to be near our extended families, and Jesse realized a long-term dream of opening his own law firm. By God's blessings, it was profitable from the get-go. During the prior year, Jesse had gotten a contract position and had also used that year researching, listening to, and reading everything about leadership and running a business. It has been so much fun to see him work hard and succeed in this venture.

It wasn't an easy journey. But we can definitely say that making short-term sacrifices in order to accomplish long-term goals can be very rewarding—especially if you're willing to stick with it when the going gets tough.

MAPPING OUT A PLAN FOR FINANCIAL FREEDOM

The financial crisis of recent years has affected most of us. Between layoffs, budget cuts, foreclosures, and the never-ending stream of bankruptcy filings, we are anxious about the state of our finances. But we don't have to live with that kind of pressure. We can overcome financial worry by purposely managing our money.

Think about this: When you put yourself in the driver's seat of your financial situation and tell your money where to go by sticking with your preplanned budget, it releases you from a major amount of stress. No longer do you have to fear whether you'll have enough money at the end of the month. No longer do you have to wonder where your money went. You have already determined exactly where each dollar you make will go so all you have to do is follow the plan.

By making wise financial decisions, money doesn't run through your fingers like sand. You'll find that you have a lot more left over to save and give!

Yes, You Need a Budget

A lot of people cringe when I bring up the word *budget*. I know, the last thing you want to do is to add something else to your plate when you already have a really full life. But once you've followed the exercises we've talked about in the first few chapters to get your priorities and time management in better shape, you should have more breathing room to allow you the time and energy to tackle a budget. And I can guarantee you the work will be worth it.

It won't be easy. In fact, it may be one of the hardest things you've ever done in your life. But I've never met anyone who has lived on a budget for a few years who has told me, "Man, I really wish we wouldn't have been careful with our money. It just ruined our lives."

Here's the beautiful thing about a budget: while it's hard and limiting at first, over time you'll realize that it's your means to enjoy life without headaches and worry. Ultimately, it's a pathway to freedom. And when you tell your money how to work for you, you can be intentional about how you use it.

Start with a Bare-bones Budget

Here are my personal recommendations on creating what I like to call a bare-bones budget. This plan will include all your basic living necessities like food, utilities, shelter, transportation, credit card bills, and so on.

Get a Handle on Your Expenses

Write down all the above budget categories, and decide how much you need to set aside every month to adequately cover all your expenses. See if you can lower any expenses by cutting your grocery bill, asking for a discount on your utilities, moving to less expensive housing, or selling your car. Any decrease in expenses will help free more money to put toward your emergency fund and to pay off debt.

Follow this budget to a tee. As much as possible, don't pay for anything that isn't a complete necessity right now. It's a short season and your sacrifices will pay off.

Build an Emergency Fund

Throw every extra penny you can toward building up your emergency fund. This will give you a cushion going forward on months that you come up short. If at all possible, I suggest including this as an expense in your budget and allocating whatever dollar amount you can afford. Increase as you go along.

Pay Off Your Debt

After your emergency fund is funded, it's time to focus all your energies on knocking out your consumer debt as quickly as possible. Continue to live on your bare-bones budget, and put everything else that you can scrounge up toward your debt.

Be as aggressive and as creative as possible in attacking your debt and getting rid of it. The sooner it's gone, the sooner you'll be able to have some breathing room in your life again. You may need to get a part-time job or sell some items you can live without. If you have some hiccups along the way—and you probably will—don't be discouraged. Stop and refund your emergency fund, if need be, and then get back to getting rid of your debt.

Create a Prioritized List of Additional Savings/Spending Goals

Finally, reevaluate your goals and track your progress on a monthly basis. If you're married, sit down with your spouse at the end of every month and discuss your finances. As you pay off debt and/or your income increases, revise your budget and create more savings and spending goals. If your debt is gone and you have a good emergency fund in place, not only will you be able to put more into savings, you'll also be able to enjoy some strategic splurging too (more on that in a bit).

Budget for Everything

One of the biggest mistakes people make when they approach budgeting is that they don't give themselves enough wiggle room. Obviously, there are times when finances are so tight, you may not have a choice. But if you have a decent income, you need to make sure that you don't make your budget categories so slim that it's too hard to stick with them. That's a surefire way to set yourself up for failure.

I was talking with a reporter from New York City not long ago, and she was asking me for specific dollar amounts for different budget categories. I explained that it's different for every family. She pressed me further, though, so I threw out some numbers for her. I told her that some people budget anywhere from twenty to one hundred dollars a month per adult for extra spending cash.

She was aghast at such low numbers and told me that she can't even walk across the street in New York City without spending ten dollars! When I asked her to explain, she began by sharing how expensive cab rates were.

"Oh," I said. "Well, then you would have a budget category for the approximate amount you'd spend on cabs each month." I went on to explain how budgeting works for us. Namely, we budget for every category that we spend in each year. If we regularly spent money on cabs, we'd budget for that. Nothing comes as a surprise. This caused her to heave a huge sigh of relief. For the first time, she realized she could live on a budget too, because it didn't mean she would never be able to spend money; a budget means she would start planning ahead of time for how she was going to spend her money.

Don't Forget the Blow Category!

In addition to budgeting for everything, we also include a category in our budget that we call "blow money." It's our extra spending category. You will probably not have one when you start budgeting on a tight income, but as you gain financial stability, I highly recommend that you include this category.

Blow money is just that—money we can blow on whatever we want to. We can also save it to make a large purchase, like my husband often does. This category is vitally important, especially for spenders who are trying to stick with a budget. (I know this because I'm married to a spender. I love him to pieces, but he's definitely cut from a different cloth than I am!)

Spenders find joy in spending money, so a budget can be restrictive to them. However, blow money can offer the freedom they crave without ruining the overall financial picture in the process. Be wise when you allot a dollar amount to this category. Don't let it defeat the purpose of a budget.

RESOURCE CENTRAL

If you've never had a budget before, I highly recommend checking out Dave Ramsey's materials and radio show (more details at DaveRamsey.com). In addition to giving you step-by-step help for getting out of debt, he offers a free online budgeting tool that walks you through the details of setting up a realistic budget.

Also, the following websites offer valuable information as well as free budgeting worksheets and software to help you develop and stick with a budget:

- ChristianPersonalFinance.com
- Mint.com
- YouNeedaBudget.com

FOLLOW-UP IS THE SUREST WAY TO FOLLOW THROUGH

As you create and follow your budget, be patient. It takes at least a few months to get the hang of it, so keep tweaking until you get it right. You'll also need to keep tweaking it as circumstances and life change.

It's important to be consistent and check in with your

progress on a monthly basis. Being accountable to someone is one of the most effective ways to get something done. You may already have an accountability partner when it comes to your career or health goals. I encourage you to do the same for your finances. Find someone who has similar goals and a comparable outlook (such as your spouse, a friend, or even an accountant) to help you stay on track. Meet regularly and review your goals. Talk about the progress you are making and the struggles you are having. Ask for his or her input and suggestions on how you can improve. Continue to follow up on a regular basis.

> Wealth consists not in having great possessions, but in having few wants.
> —EPICTETUS

SPEND SMART

Financially living with intention is not just about following helpful guidelines. It's about living out a particular mind-set. It's about learning to enjoy what you have and not compromising under societal pressures. While we've made plenty of mistakes individually and as a family, we have zero regrets that we've chosen to live beneath our means, make sacrifices, delay purchases until we can pay cash for them, and live on a strict, written budget.

To some people, not getting what you want right away or

doing without might seem like a miserable existence. But truthfully, we've found it to be the opposite. We love the peace that comes from knowing we don't have to worry about how we're going to pay for things next week or next month because we are telling our money where to go. Yes, this means that we have to delay purchases or not buy some items at all. But not having to live in fear over our financial future is worth giving up some of the things that would be nice to have. Plus, we've found there's a lot of fulfillment that comes from waiting and saving up to pay cash for something.

If you want to get and stay out of debt, save more or give more, it's likely going to mean making some sacrifices, especially in the short term. You can't change your financial situation unless you also change the way you're doing something.

You'll have to be willing to cut back, start paying cash instead of credit, eat less than gourmet meals, or not have the latest and greatest gadget or gizmo. How willing you are to make changes is directly dependent upon how motivated you are to reach your financial goals. It won't always be easy, fun, or glamorous to make short-term sacrifices. But it will be worth it, because it will put you in a position to tell your money how to work for you. You'll have the freedom to save up and pay cash for things, and to give generously to the needs in your community and around the world. And ultimately, by being wise in how you use your money, you can change lives—or even save lives. All because you didn't buy something just because you wanted it, but you planned ahead, thought about the future, and were careful in what you spent today so that you would be in a position to make a difference in lives tomorrow.

THE FORBIDDEN FRUIT OF THE SPLURGE

I'm pretty sure most of us agree that having a purpose behind our frugality gives much more meaning and motivation for saving money. However, I don't think this means we shouldn't ever splurge, that we should always buy the cheapest of everything, or that we should go without everything unnecessary lest we spend a penny more than we need to.

On the contrary, I think it's important that we have balance and breathing room in our lives—and in our budgets. If we pack our schedules so full that we never take time to stop and smell the roses, we'll likely end up rushing through life and missing out on some great moments. We'll also be frazzled, stressed, and exhausted much or all of the time.

In the same way, I believe it's important that we find a healthy balance when it comes to our finances. It's wonderful to be focused and aggressive when it comes to paying off debt or saving to pay cash for something. And it's absolutely life-changing to be in a position where you can give generously.

I also want to encourage you not to become so frugal that you forget to give yourself space in your budget to splurge strategically. If we scrimp and save so much that we never have any room to enjoy and savor life, it can lead to a miserable existence.

That said, strategic splurging doesn't have to mean spending hundreds of dollars. It could be something as simple as ordering pizza once a month with a coupon. Or browsing your favorite bookstore every other week with a latte. Or having a fun family outing. Or getting a spa treatment using a Groupon voucher.

What matters most is not how much or how little money you spend, but that you choose to splurge strategically on something that is important for your family, that you love and enjoy, or that will boost your morale and will not disrupt your frugal journey.

When you make your money work for you, you have more to work with. Budgeting for fun makes it more enjoyable because you know that going out to dinner or that occasional coffee at Starbucks is something you planned for, and it won't wreck your finances or keep you from being able to pay your electric bill.

For most of us, there will be seasons in life when our budgets are fixed because things are really tight financially. If you're in one of those seasons, don't lose heart. Constantly remind yourself that the frugal decisions you are making will ultimately pay off. And be encouraged that you are doing so much better than you would be doing if you weren't being so budget-conscious.

NOT SPENDING FOOLISHLY + SAVING = GIVING

My husband and I believe that the reason we feel fulfilled and passionate about life—even though we've made counter-cultural choices—is because frugality is a means to an end for us. If we were frugal for frugality's sake, we'd quickly burn out or give up.

For us, it's not about saving money so we can continuously upgrade our lifestyles and always be buying bigger and better things. We want to live beneath our means so that we are able to give generously to others (more on this in chapter 8!).

There's a world of need around us. The more we steward our money well, the more abundance we will have to meet those needs. The more we save, the more we have to give. Your efforts and my efforts might seem like a drop in the bucket when compared to all the need that's out there. But collectively, we can make a huge impact.

Let's live simply so that others can simply live. Because truly, there is nothing more fulfilling than living a life with outstretched arms.

GET PRACTICAL

Sit down somewhere quiet, and spend a few minutes thinking about what living financially on purpose means to you. Does it mean breaking free from debt so you can start saving for retirement? Does it mean setting aside money each month to donate to your church, a local food pantry, or another charitable organization? Does it mean setting priorities on what you spend so you have plenty of margin in your budget? Use these thoughts to create a few written, financial goals and a purpose behind those goals. Then find an accountability partner to regularly meet with and help you keep on track with your goals. And don't forget to celebrate your milestones along the way!

6 ▪▪▪▪▪▪▪▪▪▪▪▪▪▪▪▪▪▪▪▪▪▪▪▪

Manage the Home Front

And this mess is so big
And so deep and so tall,
We can not pick it up.
There is no way at all!

—DR. SEUSS, *THE CAT IN THE HAT*

Goal: Simplify and streamline your home management so you can focus your time and energy on what matters most.

Strategy: Create and implement simple, reliable systems for running your household more efficiently, smoothly planning meals, and keeping clutter at bay.

I was ready to give up my mom badge. This was just too hard. For a long time, I had looked forward to being a mom. But it certainly wasn't panning out according to my happily-ever-after plan.

My husband was gone all day. We only had one car, and Jesse needed it to get to work and school. My mom lived two and a half hours away and couldn't help as often as she would have liked because of the distance. So I was stuck in a little basement apartment, mostly by myself and with a baby who struggled to get on a regular sleep schedule.

Instead of being the amazing wife, mom, and homemaker I'd always pictured I'd be, I was having a hard time figuring out when to get a shower most days, let alone tend to the growing mountain of laundry and dust balls in the living room. I was groggy, sleep deprived, and just plain overwhelmed.

> Life is really simple, but we insist on making it complicated.
> —CONFUCIUS

KEEP IT SIMPLE

A lot has changed in my life since those early days of mothering. I now have three children and run a thriving business and blog, in addition to writing books and speaking. Have I become Superwoman? No, not in the least. I've just learned a lot of tricks to running a home efficiently. And I've become a lot more adept at multitasking, juggling, and delegating.

Most of all, I've adopted the motto Keep It Simple. Growing up, my mom had us dust the baseboards and wipe down the plant leaves with cotton balls on a monthly basis. We assumed everyone else did this too. One day, though, we discovered that wasn't the case. A friend was visiting while one of us was in the midst of the cotton-ball-plant-cleaning routine. This friend was shocked and told us she'd never even considered cleaning in such detail. Years later, I look back and wonder if maybe my mom was just trying to keep us occupied in a productive manner.

At any rate, after this revelation I decided to dial back dusting the baseboards, and I can't remember the last time I dusted our plants. I'm okay with that. (But please don't tell my mom!) Give yourself grace to let some stuff go and keep it simple. Figure out the level of orderliness and cleanliness that works for you and your family, and don't worry if it's not the same as someone else's.

In this chapter, I'm going to focus on three areas of home management that dominate most of our lives—cooking, housekeeping, and clutter management. I've found that when I have a good system for each of these tasks, it frees me up to focus my time and energy on more important things, like my best stuff list.

You may not find all three categories useful. Maybe your husband is a phenomenal cook and takes care of the meals. You may have some cleaning help or older kids who pitch in and lighten your load. Or perhaps you live alone or in such a small space that you don't need much help running your home. Use whatever valuable tools can be adopted into your unique station in life.

WHAT'S FOR DINNER?

One of the ways I incorporate my Keep-It-Simple mantra into every day is to simplify meals. If you love making time-consuming recipes and have energy and room in your schedule to do so, go for it. But if you're feeling stressed and overwhelmed, I encourage you to give yourself the freedom to keep meals simple.

In fact, if your family is okay with it, you might find it helpful to have two weeks' worth of go-to quick and easy meals that you rotate. Or you might consider taking one day a month to prepare most of the food for your main dishes for the next month to keep in the freezer.

We stick with basic meals at our home, and it works well at this season of our lives. Breakfasts are cereal or oatmeal. Lunches are leftovers, sandwiches, salads, snack foods, or macaroni and cheese. Dinners are typically some type of meat (fish, chicken, or beef), a carb (bread, rice, or potatoes), and a veggie. Or I'll make homemade pizza (takes me about fifteen minutes tops), throw together a big pot of soup, or put something in the Crock-Pot in the morning. Most of our meals can be put together in fifteen to thirty minutes, with minimal ingredients and cleanup.

I've done different things over the years, but what's currently working is to set aside time on Saturday morning to plan our menu and grocery list for the upcoming week. Then, in the afternoon, I head to the store to do the shopping. This ensures that we start the week with a full refrigerator and pantry and that we have the ingredients on hand to make the items on our menu.

Having this simple plan and giving myself the grace not to feel like I need to do more has provided me a lot of freedom from guilt. It's saved me a lot of time and energy too, which I can use to splurge on a more involved meal if I get inspired.

Here are some menu-planning tips and ideas I've found helpful:

- Use Pinterest for inspiration. I have a board on Pinterest called "Recipes I Want to Try." Every time I find a yummy-looking recipe, I pin it there. Then, when I'm planning our weekly menu, I consult this board for ideas.

- Plan meals according to what you have on hand. Save money and reduce waste by basing your menu plan on what you already have in your refrigerator and freezer. I like to use the "Ingredient Search Feature" on AllRecipes.com to generate ideas.
- Base your menu on what's in season and on sale. Check the circulars to find rock-bottom sales for that week. This will also help cut your grocery bill.
- Rotate a three-month menu plan. Consider putting together two or three months' worth of menus and corresponding grocery lists. Then just rotate these menus. I don't personally do this, but I have friends who rave about how much it simplifies their lives.

Freeze It Now; Eat It Later

While freezer cooking—preparing meals in advance and freezing them to eat at a later time—doesn't work for everyone, it has done wonders for our family. I spend a lot less time cooking and cleaning up the kitchen. I never have to worry about the question, "What's for dinner?" And it's not a huge undertaking to have guests over at the last minute or take a meal to someone.

Think you might be interested in trying your hand at freezer cooking? Here are some suggestions for a successful launch.

Start Small

If you've never done this before, start with no more than two recipes at first. You're probably capable of much more, but start small and gradually work your way up.

Choose Recipes You Love

If you want to love the recipes you freeze, make sure you pick ones you already know you or your family loves. You'll have plenty of time to experiment later, but wait until you feel confident with freezer cooking before you branch out and try a bunch of new recipes.

Set Aside Time for Cooking

Block out time during the week or on the weekend when you have a free hour and do your cooking. Give yourself a little extra time. I find sometimes it takes longer than I think it will. Rushing around trying to get things done before you have to go somewhere only sets you up for failure.

Have a Plan for Your Kids

If you have young children, make sure you plan an activity to keep them occupied. The last thing you need is to have your first freezer-cooking experience be an exercise in frustration due to constant interruptions from needy little people. The best time to do your freezer cooking might be during their afternoon naptime or after the kids go to bed.

Avoid Freezer Burn

Don't ruin your yummy food! Let it cool, wrap it well, and package it in an airtight container. These three directions are a must if you want to avoid freezer burn.

Use What You Cook in a Timely Manner

It's wonderful to have food at-the-ready in the freezer, but it does you no good if you don't actually use it. Be sure to eat it within two to three months, if not before. I always consult my freezer when planning our weekly menu and incorporate some of the meals, especially those that need to be used up soon, into our weekly menu.

Get a copy of *Not Your Mother's Make-Ahead and Freeze Cookbook* by Jessica Fisher for lots of freezer-cooking ideas, recipes, two-hour freezer-cooking plans, and more.

DON'T WANT TO SPEND ALL DAY IN THE KITCHEN? NEITHER DO I!

I love to cook and bake, but I don't have hours of time to spend in the kitchen, especially on busy weekdays. But that doesn't mean we don't enjoy home-cooked meals. I've learned to be creative and make the most of my time in the kitchen.

Here are some things that help me save time and effort.

Cook It Once; Eat It Twice

Make a big pot of soup for dinner and serve it two nights in a row. Or make two meat loaves instead of one and eat one for dinner and freeze the extra meat loaf for later. It takes a lot less time to double a recipe than it does to make it two separate times. Plus, you only have to do the dishes once.

Cook Meat in Bulk

Never cook just one pound of meat. Make it worth your while by browning multiple pounds of meat, and store the extra in the freezer. Save yourself some effort by browning it in the Crock-Pot.

Prep Your Food as Soon as You Come Home from the Store

After grocery shopping, do yourself a favor and brown the ground beef, marinate the chicken, wash and chop all the veggies, boil eggs, or do whatever it is that you're planning to do with the food you bought. Work as quickly as you can to get this done. Then go put your feet up and enjoy the feeling of knowing you've already done much of your kitchen prep work for the week.

Make Bulk Batches of Baking Mixes

Do you have certain baked goods that you like to make regularly? Take fifteen minutes on the weekends to mix a quadruple batch of the dry ingredients together. Then, when you're ready to make pancakes, cookies, or muffins, half the job is already done.

> Housekeeping ain't no joke.
> —LOUISA MAY ALCOTT

KEEPING YOUR SANCTUARY CLEAN

"Cleanliness is next to godliness." Whoever said that probably didn't have any children, a demanding job, a packed schedule, or a kitchen floor that refused to stay clean. Still, there is just something about keeping a clean and tidy environment that makes you feel better overall.

As usual, I like to stick with the basics. In our house, if we have clean laundry, sufficiently picked-up rooms, clean bathrooms, clean dishes, and relatively clean floors, I consider things to be in pretty good shape. It's never perfect, but it's usually forty-five minutes to "company ready." If someone calls me out of the blue and says he or she is stopping by, it won't take long to tidy up. All I have to do is make sure the kitchen isn't littered with dishes, the bathrooms are wiped down, and the clutter isn't dominating the space. I'm satisfied with that at this point in my life.

Five Easy Ways to Clean Up Quickly

I find that if I do the following five quick and easy tasks each day, it's a lot easier to maintain a well-ordered home. If you keep on top of these five things, you can probably accomplish them in forty-five minutes or less every day. Your home will thank you for it. And you'll feel like you did something with your day even if you don't have much else to show for your efforts!

1. Sort the mail and miscellaneous papers.
2. Do one load of laundry from start to finish.
3. Spend fifteen minutes tidying the house.
4. Wipe down the sink and toilet in each bathroom.
5. Load the dishwasher and wipe down the kitchen countertops.

FIND A CLEANING PLAN THAT WORKS FOR YOU

Do you have a cleaning plan for your home right now? Is it working? If not, consider tweaking it or trying out a new plan altogether. Sometimes a fresh change is all the motivation you need if you find yourself slacking.

The Internet is bursting with cleaning routines and inspiration. Below are three ideas that may work for you. If none seem doable, do a search for free printable cleaning routines and checklists on Google or Pinterest.

- My website offers twenty days of simple cleaning tasks to whip your house into shape. You can download a printable list or sign up for daily e-mail reminders at MoneySavingMom.com. (Search for "4 Weeks to a More Organized Home.)
- If you're motivated and enjoy making lists, you may want to check out chore planners at MotivatedMoms.com. This website provides a yearlong printable list of chores and home management tasks. It also recently released an app, if you prefer the paperless route.
- If you're not interested in planning worksheets or task lists, visit FlyLady.net to get daily e-mail reminders and ideas to help you get rid of clutter and find more order and peace in your home.

> I recently hired someone to clean my house every two weeks. I am so much less stressed out. Instead of being frazzled whenever I need to find time I don't have to clean the house, I am more relaxed because I know someone is doing it for me. My attitude has totally changed. Even my husband has noticed!
> —LAURA LEIGH

Do You Have to Do It All Yourself?

Not too long ago, I was at a moms get-together. I don't remember what we were talking about, but in the middle of the conversation, one of the moms said sheepishly, "Well, actually, I have a cleaning lady who comes every other week." She looked ashamed to admit this, but I quickly set her at ease by looking directly in her eyes and saying, "Good for you!"

We tend to think that unless we're doing every little thing to run our homes, we are failures. We beat ourselves up if we can't do it all. We feel guilty for even considering bringing in outside help on occasion. Believe me, it's necessary sometimes. If you can afford a cleaning service and it's something that will bless your family and relieve some of your anxiety, don't apologize for it!

When our third baby was born, we hired a gal from church to come over for five hours each week and help with laundry, deep cleaning, watching our children, and anything else that needed to be done. At first I struggled with guilt because I wasn't washing every piece of laundry or mopping every square inch of my kitchen floor. But I quickly got over the guilt when I realized how this freed me up to be able to breathe and love on my husband and children instead of living in a continual state of exhaustion.

WHAT YOU WANT TO KNOW

Q: I have a toddler and just had a baby. Between caring for my newborn and running after my little girl, I barely have time to brush my teeth, let alone do laundry or mop the floors. Help!

A: Accept that our lives are full of different seasons. Ideas and routines that worked in the past may not benefit us in a new season. When we're pregnant, have babies, or both, priorities shift tremendously. It isn't so easy—in fact it's nearly impossible—to plan your day and keep a super organized or spick-and-span house.

Here are some helpful tips for these joyous (and usually overwhelming) seasons:

First, lower your expectations. This is not the time for tackling big projects, signing up for ministry opportunities, or doing spring-cleaning. Stick with the basics. If your family has clean laundry and food in their bellies, the dishes are clean, and the trash is thrown out, most of the other stuff can wait.

Second, develop a simple routine (like I talked about in chapter 2). Make a basic list of five or six things you want to accomplish every day (like getting dressed, taking a shower, putting away the laundry, sorting through the mail, and sterilizing bottles). The key is "simple."

Third, give yourself grace. Don't beat yourself up over what you're not doing. Don't compare yourself to other seemingly "supermoms." Don't stress over what's not done.

Fourth, laugh often. Find the humor in every situation that you can. Surround yourself with positive people and encouraging messages to help build you up.

Fifth, don't neglect your health. Make sure you eat a nourishing diet (especially if you are a nursing mom), drink plenty of water, and take a good multivitamin. And make sleep a priority. I know how impossible this seems when you're waking up many times during the night to feed your baby. While you will probably need to give up the expectation of getting a full night's sleep for a while, sleep when you can. Even a ten- or fifteen-minute catnap can do wonders for a tired mom.

Finally, enjoy your family. Your babies are only little once. Take time to enjoy them. Stare into their faces. Soak up their cuddles and smiles and giggles and firsts. Cherish this precious time.

WHERE DID ALL THIS STUFF COME FROM?

You know one surefire way to add more time and order to your life? Get rid of excess stuff. I talked about this before, but I'll say it again. I truly believe that the less you have, the less time you spend on upkeep, maintenance, and cleaning. Either you control the clutter or the clutter will control you.

I admit, when it comes to clutter, my attitude is ruthless. My husband and I have adopted a minimalist lifestyle because we've found this is the environment that we work best in and that keeps our lives simple. Our house is pretty bare. Outside of necessary furniture like couches, tables, beds, and dressers, there's not much else. Only a few knickknacks. A lot of blank wall space. To some, our house might look too empty, but we truly love it.

A little extreme? Maybe. But I like the benefits. I don't spend a lot of time looking for lost articles under piles of stuff. I don't have to dust and move around extra things. Our space is easy to keep clean. And I find that I'm more productive when things are orderly and clutter-free.

Take One Step (or Room) at a Time

If you feel overwhelmed with clutter, don't panic. Instead, create a realistic plan of attack. Take one room at a time, and commit to working on it for fifteen minutes five days each week until it's finished. Then start on the next.

Once you figure out what you are keeping and what you are getting rid of, make a space for items that seem to stick out like a sore thumb in a room. If you don't assign a place for everything, it's going to sit out, become clutter, and accumulate some more.

For example, if you have an overflowing pile of magazines in your living room and you've determined to keep them, put them in a magazine rack or decorative crate. If your bathroom counters are littered with hair and skin products, put them under the sink or in a medicine cabinet. We use plastic tubs to store things like DVDs, CDs, medicines, and crafts. Any type of storage container is great to keep items more organized, but make sure that you're actually using the items that are in that storage container!

An important key to maintaining a clutter-free environment is to monitor your purchases. By now, you should have a financial plan in place that doesn't allow for excess spending. If you're on the fence of buying an item, ask yourself if you have the space for it. If not, are you willing to make room for it or get rid of something else in its place? Is the item a true necessity? Will it create more clutter?

> Cleaning your house while your kids are still growing is like shoveling the walk before it stops snowing.
>
> —PHYLLIS DILLER

A SLOB COMES CLEAN

If you struggle with hanging on to stuff and don't know where to start, you need to meet my friend Dana, who blogs at ASlobComesClean.com. She's a reformed pack rat whose life changed when she finally came to terms with her disorganized nature and figured out what worked for her and her personality.

I asked her if she'd be willing to let me interview her for this book. Read on to find out about her eye-opening experience.

ME. How has being purposeful in managing your house alleviated stress for you?

DANA. Before I began what I call my "deslobification" process, my biggest source of stress was my bewilderment over the state of my home. I was constantly frustrated that no matter how hard I tried, the house continually went back to being a disaster.

For instance, if I was hosting a party and cleaned up the house, I'd think, This is how I like my house to look! Three days later my house was as messy as ever. Over the past several years, I've developed habits that specifically help me combat my slob tendencies. As long as I keep up with those habits, my home stays under control. Even when I get consumed with a huge, creative project and my house spirals back into disaster, I'm no longer bewildered. I know exactly what to do to get right back on track.

ME. Has getting your home in order helped you to be able to have time to focus on more important things?

DANA. When kitchen counters are piled with dirty

dishes and you can't use the dining room table because it's covered in stuff, there's a constant sense of nagging guilt. Making dinner is more difficult. Craft projects with the kids get put off indefinitely because you don't have time to declutter the table and do the project.

By focusing on one small daily task at a time, I began to see the value in habits. Doing three or four simple things every day had more of an impact on my home than daylong damage control sessions. I also began to see how little time it took to do the dishes every single night (even if there didn't seem to be enough to be worthwhile) compared to spending an entire day excavating the kitchen. Massive amounts of decluttering meant surfaces stayed clearer, and I could act on those wonderful, unpredictable, teachable moments with the kids.

Toy Overload

Something happens when you have children. Toys are everywhere. Your home can quickly get hijacked by colorful blocks, plastic figures, puzzle pieces, chewed-on books, and game pieces. Think *Toy Story* in every room. Your leather ottoman with intricate stitching and artfully crafted wooden legs is unnoticeable under the towering piles of board games, stuffed animals, and Play-Doh, some of which have left permanent stains. Even though before you had your little ones, you promised yourself your home would not become a toy jungle, it happened. Well, you can't always win with good intentions, but you can succeed with a plan.

The fact is, having children means your home will be filled

with playthings. It comes with the territory. However, this doesn't mean your house has to be your toddler's domain with all his or her fluffy, noisy, bouncy subjects taking up residence in every nook and cranny. We've chosen to limit toys in our home because we want to raise children who are content and don't feel like they have to have the latest and greatest of everything. Of course, the added bonus is that it helps to minimize clutter.

Whether your child has a few or a ton of toys, here are ways to help you maintain a sense of order when it comes to accumulating and organizing his or her playthings.

Be Choosy

Stick with quality, versatile toys. We enjoy things like LEGOs, blocks, Melissa & Doug toys, dolls, tool sets, educational toys, and arts and crafts. We try to have toys that encourage creativity rather than solely entertain.

If It's Not Regularly Played With, Don't Keep It

There's no point in keeping something around if no one likes it or uses it on a regular basis. Has a toy sat in the corner untouched for weeks? Is it broken? Does it have parts that can't be replaced? Get rid of it. If it's still in great condition but it's just not being played with regularly, consider passing it on to another family who might use it. Better yet, set up a quarterly toy swap with friends to exchange toys you no longer need or use. Everyone comes home with new toys—all for free!

Focus on Contentment Versus Consumerism

Purposefully keeping toys simple at our house and focusing on quality time with our children are two ways we hope to instill contentment in their hearts, a quality that will benefit them for the rest of their lives. We live in a consumer-driven society where people spend much of their lives working to climb the ladder of success. They want to be the best, have the best, buy the best, and look the best. There's nothing wrong with working hard to accomplish a particular goal, but there is something wrong when we attach our self-worth and value on how much or what we have. Children need love and nurturing more than things. This point cannot be reiterated enough. Money can't buy love. All the stuff in the world will never replace a relationship with your child. And remember, building memories is so much more important than buying toys.

KEEPING TRACK OF DAY-TO-DAY HOME TASKS

Without a plan, you don't know where you're supposed to go or what you're supposed to do. I encourage you to set aside time in your schedule each week to make a simple home management plan of action as well as goals for the coming week. Reviewing this weekly list of goals is always so encouraging because even on those weeks when it feels like nothing got done, I'll realize that I did in fact accomplish some things. Seeing progress made is a great feeling.

In addition, I've found that having a daily homemaking plan gives me freedom, saves me a great deal of time, and brings peace and order into our home. I can focus on the task at hand because I know the other tasks will get taken care of during their designated time in the day.

For instance, I can walk past the pile of laundry on my bed

at noon because I know that I have a time slot at 4 p.m. to do it. I rarely stress out over "what's for dinner?" at 5 p.m. because I try to plan for dinner right after lunch—throwing the ingredients for the stew in the Crock-Pot, making dough for rolls in my bread machine, or setting out the meat to thaw.

How I Plan My Week

About seven years ago while I was reading through blogs, I discovered the concept of a "homemaking binder." The bloggers who had these were very organized women and loved spreadsheets, details, lists, and charts. I figured since their homemaking binders were working so well for them, I should create one that mirrored theirs. So I spent a lot of time researching, printing forms, and compiling an elaborate homemaking binder system.

The problem was, since I like to keep things simple, my big binder with a section and printable for just about every area of my life was too much. Too tedious. Too overwhelming. Too complicated. Instead of helping me, the detailed system hindered me because it bogged me down and constantly made me feel guilty if I wasn't checking everything off all the lists in all the sections.

By trying to make someone else's complicated system work for me, I ended up frustrated. And more than that, I felt like a failure because I couldn't seem to make the homemaking binder work well for me when it seemed to work so well for others.

In the end, I realized that I needed to be who God had created me to be instead of working so hard to make someone else's system work for me. I ended up creating a really simple binder, with just a few sections, and that has worked well for me.

Here is a list of the pages I use.

My Goals for the Week Page

On this page, I list ten goals I have for the week in four different categories: family, personal, homemaking, and business. I limit myself to ten goals total so that it's more realistic and doable. I rarely get every goal crossed off, but by having intention in how I approach my week, it helps me plan each day with more purpose and get more things that matter done versus spending much of my week putting out fires. I post my goals and progress every Monday on my blog as public accountability to keep me on track. If you don't have a blog, you can e-mail these goals to a friend or post them on your fridge or cubicle at work.

My Daily Docket Page

I fill one of these out every night before I go to bed (see the Daily Docket in the appendix). This page tells me what I need to accomplish the next day, and it has sections to track things I need to buy and what I'm making for dinner. You could create your own form or system by writing these things on a notebook page or a to-do list on your phone each day. Or feel free to download one of the home management forms I use (they are customizable and are available under the "Free Printables" tab on my website).

My Weekly Menu

I type up our menu on the computer each week and print it out. Since I'm already making the menu to post on my blog each Monday, I just print that out and stick it in my binder. You could also post this on your fridge or have it on your smartphone instead of putting it in your binder.

Weekly and Monthly Cleaning Lists

I also have weekly and monthly cleaning lists where I track what regular cleaning and deep cleaning I need to do each week and month. I have these lists available under the "Free Printables" section of my website. If you find them helpful, you can customize and print them to use in your own home.

On Saturday (or sometimes it doesn't happen until Monday morning!), I sit down and map out my menu plan, grocery list, blogging projects and posts, weekly to-dos, and goals for the following week, including cleaning. I review my monthly and yearly goals at this time to help me in planning. I divvy up the things that need to be done over the course of the week to specific days. The night before each day, I fill out the daily page with my to-do list for the next day. Then each day I look at my daily page to see what I need to do and cross off tasks as I complete them. At the end of the day, I transfer unfinished tasks to the following day.

Google Calendar Keeps Our Whole Family Organized

In addition to the pages in my home management binder, I use Google calendar to track all outings, events, appointments, and project deadlines. I consult it at the end of the week when making my goals list for the following week. I also consult my Google calendar every evening when making my daily list for the next day.

One thing I love about Google calendar is that you can merge multiple calendars. So my husband and I have our calendars shared so I can see what appointments and things he has going on each day, and he can see the same for me. I also have calendars for different blogging projects and other business items. I love that I can see all the calendars at once if I want to get a broad picture of my entire week at a glance. Or I can choose to see one or two calendars at a time.

It's About Teamwork

No one person should be responsible for every task, chore, or project in running a home. Can you imagine if you did every bit of cleaning, cooking, organizing, bill paying, yard maintenance, shopping, and (go ahead, fill in the blank!) entirely on your own? Or maybe you do. If so, I'm willing to bet you are worn out and exhausted! I know I would be.

My husband and I are firm believers in families being a team. Each individual member should pitch in and bear the weight of running a household to the level of his or her ability. Now, I know I am very, very blessed to be married to a man who doesn't shirk when it comes to work—whether that's in his professional role as an attorney or when he's dealing with a clogged toilet. He works from sunup to sundown and then some. I'm constantly challenged by his discipline and work ethic. I often tell him, "Would you stop making me feel so lazy?"

My husband and I are a team through and through, and we both contribute to our family economically as well as by keeping up our home, training our children, and managing our household. If your husband works long hours or travels, you are going to have much different family dynamics. However, if you're married and feeling like you are shouldering too heavy of a load, I urge you to talk openly with your family members about how to shift some of that load elsewhere so that it doesn't crush you.

For those of you who are single moms, can I encourage

you to give yourself grace? You've got a lot on your plate. Keep up with what's most important and let the other stuff go. Make sure the bathrooms are regularly cleaned, the kitchen is semi-presentable at least a few times per week, and everyone has clean clothes to wear and food to eat. If you've got the time, tackle a few deep-cleaning projects one or two weekends a month. If not, don't worry about it. Know that it's more important that you and your kids sleep well, eat, and breathe right now.

Whether you're married or single, if you have children, can I encourage you to make it a priority to teach them to be assets to your family? While we very much want our children to enjoy their childhood and revel in that carefree state, we also feel that one of the greatest gifts we can instill in them is a strong work ethic. We have found that modeling hard work, practicing servanthood, and having them work alongside us from an early age have been great teaching tools. We give them age-appropriate chores to accomplish each day and encourage them to take initiative in helping outside of their daily chore list. We try to make it fun and exciting, and we've been amazed at how much our children can really be a help, even at a young age.

REMEMBER WHAT I'VE SAID ABOUT PERFECTION?

Though I try to maintain as much order as I can in my home, I've realized that it's okay if everything isn't perfect or even close to perfect. Life is full of disruptions, messes, and curveballs. At different times in your life, you're going to need to put more energy and effort into some things while other things will need to be put on the back burner for the time being. Something's always going to be somewhat out of balance.

Having a plan for my day has helped me tremendously, but my schedule doesn't roll smoothly all the time. There are unexpected interruptions, unintentional spills, children with bad attitudes, and random disruptions to each day. I used to beat myself up that I wasn't as organized and efficient as I wanted to be. But I started realizing a woe-is-me attitude is unproductive and discouraging.

I'm slowly learning to give myself grace. When I'm tired, I'm learning to choose sleep over a spotlessly clean kitchen. When I'm feeling burned out, I'm learning to let myself not worry about blogging or laundry for a few hours and instead do something fun with my children, my husband, or a friend. Life is meant to be enjoyed and savored, not run through at breakneck speed. Take time to stop and smell the roses, even if it means fewer things get crossed off the to-do list!

GET PRACTICAL

One of the best ways to manage the home front is to get rid of clutter. By now, you know it's one of my favorite things to do. Here's a challenge for you. For the next four weeks, I'd like you to pick one room a week to declutter.

Week 1: Tackle Your Kitchen

Go through the kitchen cupboards, pantry, under the sink, stockpile shelves, and any other closets or cupboards in your kitchen, and then ruthlessly clear out any and all clutter and unnecessary items you find. Consider passing on extra food and household items to friends or donating these to someone in need.

Week 2: Declutter Your Master Bedroom

Go through your master bedroom, including the closet and the dressers. Make piles of your clothes to be donated, given away to friends, or added to your garage sale bins.

Week 3: Sweep Through the Bathrooms

Throw out expired medicines, lotions/creams/shampoos you haven't used for over a year, and old magazines and catalogs from months ago (yeah, I know they're in there).

Week 4: Focus on the Living Room and Hallway Closets

Do the same things you've done for each room in the past three weeks. Clear the clutter. Get rid of it, store it if necessary, donate it, or place it in the garage sale bin.

7

When You Feel Like a Failure

Never give up, for that is just the place and time that the tide will turn.
—HARRIET BEECHER STOWE

> **Goal**: See failures and disappointments as stepping-stones rather than stumbling blocks.
>
> **Strategy**: Learn to stop negative self-talk and transform those reminders into powerful, positive truths about who I am as a person.

Sipping a piping hot drink at the local coffee shop, my friend looked up unexpectedly and said, "I want to ask you something." I could tell it was hard for her to get the question out but that she was desperately looking to me for an answer. "What do you do when you want to give up?"

I could see the look of disappointment in her eyes. She went on to explain how she'd poured herself into a project this past year, did everything she knew to make it succeed, and it was going nowhere. Discouraged and disheartened, she felt like all her efforts were in vain. My dear friend was on the verge of giving up.

Immediately, my heart ached for her. I've been where she was. Investing so much into something only to feel like all your time and energy was a waste is tough. Really tough.

It reminded me of one of the hardest years in my marriage. As I shared in chapter 5, when my husband graduated law school, he endured some career disappointments that shook the very foundation of our marriage. The months when he was out of work after being asked to resign were almost unbearable. Jesse was already beaten up, exhausted, and discouraged. He felt like a colossal failure. My battle with postpartum depression in the midst of this dark time didn't help matters much. We were both stressed, exhausted, and overwhelmed—and trying to keep together a marriage that seemed to be falling apart.

> Things don't go wrong and break your heart so you can become bitter and give up. They happen to break you down and build you up so you can be all that you were intended to be.
> —CHARLIE "TREMENDOUS" JONES

Jesse and I can look back at that difficult time in our lives and realize that while it was hard, we both grew so much as a result. Here's what he has to say about it:

When we married, Crystal and I sort of had our lives all mapped out and planned out. We were sure of ourselves, determined, and arrogant. When all your plans and hopes and dreams are stripped away from you, it's humbling. But hitting rock-bottom was exactly what we both needed.

We learned to have compassion for others. We learned to stop thinking we had it all together (because we found out we didn't!). And we realized how much we had to be grateful for.

We also learned to rely upon the Lord more than ever and to live life with open hands—willing to do whatever He called us to and be whatever He wanted us to be, even if His plans for us looked totally different from what we thought they were supposed to look like.

The lessons we learned through these life failures strengthened our marriage. We learned a lot more about each other. Weathering the storms of life together deepened our roots and our love for each other.

As I mentioned, two amazing things came as a result of that hard time—Jesse started his own law practice, and I launched MoneySavingMom.com. We truly believe that neither of these businesses would have happened had we not experienced the heartache, failure, and disappointment of that trying time.

I could relate to my friend's question, having been in places in the past ten years when I really wanted to give up. I encouraged her to consider whether her project was something she was passionate about and that she felt God was calling her to. She said it was, so I encouraged her not to give up, even though it might seem like her hard effort was going nowhere. Who knows? Maybe something big was about to happen. Or maybe the perseverance she was learning was going to open up other new opportunities for her in the future.

Whatever the case, my challenge to her was this: When the going gets tough, it's hard to stick it out and stick with it.

Running away or quitting is often an easier way to cope. But ignoring or hiding from our situations will never fix anything.

UNABLE TO MOVE

If you want to change your life, you have to be willing to take the first step. I've already equipped you with some basic, life-transforming tools to effectively manage your time, make some goals, and learn self-discipline. You may be gung ho and making some major changes to start living on purpose. Or you may be ankle-deep in the water, afraid to dive in or get totally wet. You even may have made some significant headway, but something—an event, a fear, a failure, an insecurity—has caused you to lose your footing and become stagnant.

Feeling stuck is hard. It's amazing how much weight it can carry and how powerful it can seem when you don't feel like you're getting anywhere and every time you turn around, another curveball is thrown your way. Giving up on the desires and goals you have created to start living intentionally can be tempting, especially if so much time has passed and you haven't seen the results you want. Maybe you have committed to losing fifty pounds and the scale has barely budged in weeks. Maybe you have carefully followed your financial savings plan, but losing your job (and not being able to find one in months) threw a wrench in your goals. Maybe you have been working on that business idea for longer than a year without seeing any profits or evidence of growth.

It seems you'll never be able to get unstuck. When you struggle for a long time and are barely getting by, it can be easy to call off the whole thing and forget about your dreams, goals, and desires, or making any improvements in your life. But if there's one thing I've learned, it's this: if you stop focusing on your goals or where you want to go in life, you'll never make any progress.

So dream big dreams. Stick with your goals. Don't give up hope. Don't believe for a second that a small step in the right direction is a pointless exercise. As long as you have breath in your body, opportunity is waiting for you somewhere.

> I am not discouraged because every wrong attempt discarded is a step forward.
> —THOMAS EDISON

WHAT IF I FAIL?

The big presentation at work that you prepared months for didn't go as smoothly as you expected. Your home organization project flopped. The holiday party you've spent months planning turned into a disaster.

It's okay. Failing doesn't make you a failure; it makes you human.

Failure is inevitable. Ouch! Even though this reality might sting, the truth is, you are going to fail in life. At some point. At something. Failure isn't proof that you're a loser, a mess-up, or someone who will never get it together. On the contrary, failure is evidence that you're trying. And you know what shows even more grit? When you try again—after you've failed.

I'm not the only one who thinks failure is to be expected.

A guy I know is currently working for a start-up company that is actively seeking funding. The other day I was chatting with him about the process, and he mentioned an interesting fact. He said that investors aren't concerned with whether you have started many successful companies; what they really care about is whether you've failed in some of your ventures. Why? They want to see that you have the courage to try again after failure. This is one of the biggest qualities they look for when considering what compares and which projects to invest in.

If you're living life to your fullest potential, taking risks, and trying new things, failing at something is unavoidable. We aren't always going to be able to do everything well, nor will every idea we have turn into a golden opportunity.

WHAT YOU CAN DO WHEN YOU FAIL

Getting stuck, stagnant, or overwhelmed by missing the mark doesn't mean we are lost causes. We can still live on purpose even when we mess up, stumble, or fall flat on our faces.

Failure doesn't define you—unless you let it. You can choose to wallow in despair over the fact that you failed at something, or you can choose to get up, dust yourself off, and move forward. It may not be easy to do, especially if your heart is bruised by disappointment, but it's the surest way to continue your journey to live on purpose.

There are three big lessons I've learned when it comes to failure: I can learn from my experience, failure can be my friend, and I have to keep moving forward or my goals will fall to the wayside.

> Sometimes adversity is what you need to face
> in order to become successful.
> —ZIG ZIGLAR

Learn from the Experience

The biggest key to help you face your failure is to use the experience as a teachable moment. Ask yourself, Why? Why did that project not succeed? Why didn't I achieve my goal? Why did I lose money on that business idea? Why did my book proposal not sell? Why did I fail that exam? Why did profits go down?

You can't come up with a solution until you isolate the problem. Spend some time evaluating your outcome. If you have a mentor or know someone who was in a similar situation, seek out his or her advice. Someone with more experience may be able to shed light on some possible missteps and figure out how you can rectify the problem.

There are many reasons for failure. Maybe you went about something the wrong way. Or you set unrealistic goals in the first place. Or you didn't have enough experience or knowledge to follow through. And sometimes things just don't pan out.

I had the opportunity to talk to Phil Vischer, known for creating the popular animated kids' video series VeggieTales. He shared with me the lessons he learned about taking the nosedive from great success to losing it all and how happy he is today. Here's what he said:

> In 1990, I was a starving artist, a newlywed animator with
> a ten-second clip of a computer-generated cucumber and

tomato, wondering how on earth I could bring my ideas to life and make an impact for the glory of God. I prayed, and I trusted Him. Ten years later I was well on my way to seeing my dream come true. By that time, my business partner and I had sold more than thirty million VeggieTales videos. I was building a Christian Disney.

Three years later I was sitting in a bankruptcy courtroom, watching as everything I had built was packed into a box and sold to the highest bidder. My dream had died and I hadn't a clue why. I wondered why God would let this happen, especially to a dream that I believed was God-inspired.

Over the next year, I felt in my heart His answer. The truth was, I had become miserable in relentlessly pursuing my dream at the expense of my health, my family, my employees—everything. I had made the work I was doing more important than my relationship with God. My life was not focused on finding fulfillment in God alone, but in making an impact. And all the while, I had turned into a crazed executive cranking out children's videos while working himself to death. I had to learn to let go of my dreams and hold on to God. And boy, am I happier this way!

Failure Can Be Your Friend

Failure is not glamorous. It's not fun. And it won't usually win you any accolades. Despite this, I have come to believe that failure is my friend. Through failure, I've discovered weaknesses and shortcomings in my life. I've pinpointed character flaws that I need to work on. And I've uncovered many, many ways to do things that don't work.

I wouldn't have chosen all the failures I've experienced in

life, but in retrospect, learning invaluable lessons the hard way has helped me. I've developed more as a person, reshaped the way I approach challenges in life, and grown into a better wife, mother, friend, and business owner.

Instead of running from failure, take time to examine what you can learn from it so that you don't make the same mistakes again. By doing so, you'll probably agree with me that failure can become your greatest teacher to propel you onward and upward!

> It does not matter how slowly you go so long as you do not stop.
> —CONFUCIUS

Keep Moving Forward

If you've failed in the past, it's easy to convince yourself it's not worth trying again because you'll probably fail. Do not let the fear of failure keep you from taking a step in the direction of success. Even if you do end up stumbling, falling, or struggling, you'll still be much further along than if you never started at all.

Few people know that MoneySavingMom.com was not my first try at a frugal-living website. Wonder why you never hear about my first frugal-living website? Because it never went anywhere. Yes, that's right. To put it more accurately, it completely flopped.

While I was pregnant with our second child and my husband was looking for work, I spent the better part of two months brainstorming, creating content, and building SimplyCentsible .com. I envisioned having a whole series of frugal e-books that

I'd sell, offering money-saving articles and linking to other e-books and affiliate programs.

I'd dabbled in blog monetization and e-bookselling enough to know that it was possible to make a decent side income from a site like this. Plus, I'd recently met a family who was earning fourteen hundred dollars per month off of Google advertising on their frugal-living site. My hopes were high. I wanted this venture to produce enough money for our family to live off of, if need be.

I poured my time and energy into setting up this website, eager to see how well it was going to do. When it was finally ready to launch, I excitedly announced it on the mommy blog I had then, hoping for an explosion of traffic.

It never came. A few visitors trickled in, nowhere near the amount of traffic I was confident the site would attract. And I don't believe I ever earned even a penny from it. I finally shut it down after a few months.

But a seed was planted.

A year later, the time was right and I tried again—this time starting a blog instead of a website and focusing on giving people practical, step-by-step handholding to get their finances in order. I'm so glad I didn't give up after the first time, because I would have missed out on so many amazing opportunities as a result.

COMPARISON IS THE THIEF OF JOY

"I'll never be good enough."

"I'm not as smart as she is."

"I'll never be able to wear that dress/save money/go back to school/start my own business."

I think we, as women, are our worst critics. Comparison is one of the biggest traps to losing our momentum or giving up before we even start our journeys to say goodbye to survival mode. It's easy to want what we don't have or see something better in others that we lack ourselves.

Here's a secret: no one has it all together. Everyone has struggles and difficulties. But I've learned how important it is to love, appreciate, and respect ourselves and extend grace and kindness to ourselves when we feel inadequate.

Recently, as I was perusing through blogs, I stumbled upon this beautiful one written by an even more beautiful woman. As I read her posts, I began to feel inadequate, ugly, disorganized, and out of shape compared to her. She was pretty, in shape, creative, witty, and had a gorgeous home with more children than I do. She seemed to have it all together. I kept on reading and continued to feel even worse.

Then I landed on a post where she talked about this one particular woman she admired and wanted to be like. Imagine my shock when I clicked on the link and discovered the woman she was referring to was me!

Yes, this woman whom I felt I paled in comparison to wanted to be like me. And here I was, secretly wishing I were her. In that moment, I realized just how silly it was to play the comparison game.

Comparison only leads to discontentment. We put ourselves down. We feel badly. Nothing good can come from it.

When we are focused on what we cannot change, we cannot make the most out of who we are and what we have to offer. We can't appreciate our journeys or the beauty that surrounds us. We can't live with gratitude. We can't even live on purpose because we're stuck in wishful thinking. We can, however, choose to be intentional in how we live our lives by making the most of all that we've been given instead of wishing we were someone else.

WHAT YOU WANT TO KNOW

Q: So many of my friends and women I know who have children have work-from-home businesses. I don't. I don't feel I have the time while caring for four kids. But I still feel pressured to provide for my family because it seems everyone else is. What should I do?

A: I started working at home out of necessity; I now do it because I enjoy it and because it gives me the opportunity to help hundreds of thousands of families across America while not neglecting my most important priorities as a wife and mom.

You need to do what works for your own family. While I believe every woman should seek to be a home economist, I have never and will never say that every woman should work from home at every season in her life. In my blog, I share things on working from home because I want to encourage women who have time and are struggling financially to be creative and find ways to bring in extra income.

However, if you're overwhelmed with your life, I encourage you to focus on streamlining and bringing order and structure into your home so you can enjoy your children and bless your husband. You don't need to

add something else to your plate right now. Be encouraged and love on those little ones of yours.

How to Get Out of the Comparison Game

How can we avoid being a victim of our insecurities and
stop comparing our looks, efforts, or results to others? Here are
a few tips.

Set Goals According to Your Own Ability

For a number of years, we've taken an annual vacation with
all my extended family to a lake resort. We stay in rustic cabins
near the lake and spend most of each day on the water taking
turns skiing, tubing, and swimming. It's always a wonderful time
of making memories, getting sunburns, and making myself try
waterskiing yet again.

Unlike most of the rest of my family, I'm not a great water
skier. In fact, I have yet to successfully slalom, despite repeated
tries to get up almost each and every year. But every year I make
myself at least get out there and do it once or twice, just to challenge myself in an area that I'm not strong in.

Last year, instead of the usual repeated attempts at slalom-
ing I typically do, I decided to play it safe and just waterski with
two skis. It doesn't look anywhere near as cool or sophisticated
as waterskiing with one, but at least it allows me to get and stay
up for a while without having repeated crash landings.

My goal was simple: get up on two skis, stay up, go over
both wakes and back again, and drop the rope before falling.
Yes, I know; it probably seems pathetic to those of you who are

seasoned skiers, but to me accomplishing this goal was a fairly big feat.

As I was out on the lake on two skis looking quite incompetent and uncoordinated, I was reminded of how important it is for each of us to set goals that are realistic for us and our own abilities. If I were to focus on how microscopic my skiing goals were in light of someone else's, I could easily become discouraged.

But I'm not someone else. I'm me. My talents and abilities are going to differ wildly from the person next to me. I can either accept and embrace this or spend my life feeling like I don't measure up.

We need to set goals—financial, personal, relationship, health—that are in line with our individual abilities, gifts, situations, and strengths. If we set ones that are far-fetched and unattainable, we'll live our entire lives feeling like failures. When we are seeking to live on purpose, it's vitally important that we keep focused on ourselves, not on our sister, our best friend, our neighbor, or the "perfect" blogger.

If I were to set a goal to be hired as a professional waterskier next year, I'd be setting myself up for defeat. In the same way, maybe you aren't in a position to pay off five thousand dollars' worth of credit card bills this year. Who cares that your neighbor may be able to pay off all her debt in six months and you have only paid off 10 percent of yours? You are not in her situation and vice versa.

> Do what you can, with what you have, where you are.
> —THEODORE ROOSEVELT

Focus on your own progress. Remember, it doesn't matter how well you're doing compared to someone else, but that you're giving it your best shot!

Don't Hold Yourself Up to Someone Else's Standard

I believe much of our feelings of failure are not truly failure at all. They are feelings of inadequacy that come as a result of comparing ourselves to other people.

What works well for one person doesn't always work for someone else. So instead of beating yourself up for "failing," accept the fact that it might be a fantastic idea for others, but it just wasn't the best thing for you.

Not too long ago, a friend e-mailed me to ask if I'd run a half marathon with her in five months. My knee-jerk reaction was, "Are you kidding me?" In fact, I wrote her back and said, "You're kind to ask, but I'm still working on trying to consistently run five to six miles without stopping. I don't think I'll be anywhere near ready to run a half marathon in five months."

For some of you athletic types, you're probably shaking your head wondering why I'd turn down the opportunity when I had a good chunk of time to train. But remember my story of how running isn't something that has come easily for me? In fact, it's taken me months of hard work and effort to finally be at a place where I can run six miles without thinking I'm going to die. Yes, someday I hope to be able to run a half marathon. But I know myself and my abilities well enough to know that trying to train for a half marathon, even a few months out, would be pushing myself too hard, too fast.

Be Kind to Yourself

We got home last Sunday night, exhausted from spending a long day at church, an event, and dinner with my extended family. It had been a full weekend. I mentioned something to my husband about how I'd love to just lie in bed and read for a little while, but I couldn't because I really needed to get the house cleaned up. He looked at me and said, "When are you ever going to learn to give yourself grace? You've had a busy weekend and you have a full week ahead. Go lie down and enjoy your book. I'll clean up the house."

Two things are obvious from this story: (1) I married a good man. Oh yes, I did. (2) I'm still working on learning to be kind to myself.

Know this: you're never going to be perfect. You're never even going to be close to perfect. Accept this and be encouraged with any progress you make. Look ahead and focus on the future instead of feeling frustrated or upset over what you can't change.

In addition, don't allow yourself to hash and rehash situations where you feel like you messed up. For instance, if you need to apologize to someone for something you did wrong, go apologize. Don't dwell on your mistake. Learn from the experience and then move on.

WHAT ARE YOUR GIFTS?

Take a few minutes and think about some of the personality traits, qualities, gifts, talents, and characteristics you really admire about yourself. Maybe you are naturally self-disciplined, compassionate, or hardworking. Maybe you are gifted in music, entrepreneurship, or writing.

Whatever these gifts are, write them down in the space below. Refer to this list when you are struggling with comparing yourself to someone else. Focus on what you like, admire, and appreciate about yourself. And stop worrying about what you don't have that someone else does.

_____

_____

_____

_____

_____

_____

Get Rid of the Lies and Start Believing the Truth

Remove from your vocabulary sentences that start with, "I can't . . . ," "I'll never be able to . . . ," and "I'm not good enough at . . ." These words don't set you up for success. They only trap you in eventual defeat.

Here's a challenge. For the next twenty-four hours, keep track of all the negative self-talk that not only comes out of your mouth but also runs through your mind. Be mindful of what you say to yourself and write those things down.

You may be sitting in front of your computer trying to beat the clock and meet a deadline and thinking, *I'm so slow. I wish I was as productive as Jenn. I'll never be able to finish this on time.* Whatever the thought, write it down. At the end of twenty-four hours, take some time and review your list. I bet you'll be surprised at how much space that negativity takes in your mind.

Once you're aware of your negative thoughts, you have to replace them with positive ones. You can't just stop thinking bad things; you have to focus on speaking out the good—the wonderful talents and abilities you do have.

Negative Comparison	Positive Reinforcement
These cookies are horrible. I'll never be as good of a baker as Amber.	God has given me so many unique talents. I'll just do the best I can with these cookies.
Patty is so much thinner than I am and she doesn't even have to work out. I'm a fat blob.	I'm working on becoming healthier every day and am taking better care of the body God gave me.
I don't know why they asked me to be on the guest panel. I'm not even smart. What am I going to say?	I have so much to offer with my life experience and perspective. I'm thankful to be able to use my knowledge any way I can.
All my friends seem to be doing such an amazing job in their mothering. They are so organized and do all these fun things with their kids. I feel like I'm such a failure as a mom.	I might not be as organized as some of my friends and I might not be great at planning fun crafts to do, but I can have fun with my kids by playing with them, listening to them, and laughing with them.

If you struggle with appreciating who you are and often compare yourself with others, I recommend you read *A Confident Heart* by Renee Swope and *You're Already Amazing* by Holley Gerth. These authors share their stories of insecurity and how they have overcome that unwinnable game.

ON THE VERGE OF GIVING UP?

If you have stumbled or fallen flat on your face in your journey, I don't want you to stay stuck. You don't need to give up. You don't need to throw in the towel. You don't need to beat yourself up for not being able to handle it, get it, or achieve it.

Life happens, the unexpected comes up, and things are not going to go along smoothly all the time. When you hit a rough patch, have a disruption to your normal schedule, or are up all night with a sick child, don't feel frustrated that you got off track. This won't do anything to help you. It will likely only make matters worse.

When things get off track, don't wallow in self-pity or give up on yourself. Focus on doing the best you can. I had to remind myself of this recently. I had just started a new routine for our homeschooling and things were going so well. Then *bam*! Four out of the five of us came down with the flu. And this wasn't any old flu. This was the knock-you-down-and-lay-you-flat-for-six-days flu.

It meant that the schedule that had been running so beautifully was completely shelved for survival. As I was lying in bed feeling miserable, I had a hard time not feeling discouraged over all the days that were ticking by with little or nothing to show for them.

Then I reminded myself, "Hey, we're alive, my kids are well cared for, I'm getting the rest I need so I can recover, and everything else can wait. It will be okay." Instead of focusing on what wasn't getting done, I started thinking of all the things my kids and I could do that we wouldn't usually get to do. We played games while lying on the floor. We looked at photo albums.

We watched movies together. We listened to audiobooks. We flipped through picture book after picture book. I also got in some extra writing while lying in bed next to sleeping children (an added bonus!).

Changing my attitude from beating myself up over a situation I couldn't control to trying to make the most of it turned our sickness into a really memorable experience—even if we still had our share of feeling miserable.

> Joy is what happens when we allow ourselves to recognize how good things really are.
> —MARIANNE WILLIAMSON

GET PRACTICAL

Have you experienced failure? Are you just coming out of a situation that you spent a lot of time on, sacrificed for, and worked tirelessly on, but it didn't work out? Instead of getting hung up on the mistakes you've made or circumstances that were simply out of your control, consider the following:

- What can you learn from your experience? What valuable lesson can it teach you?
- Was there anything you could have done to avoid failure? Why or why not?
- How can you move from feeling stuck to gaining momentum, even if it's only one step forward?

8

Yes, You Can Make a Difference

No one is useless in this world who lightens the burdens of another.
—CHARLES DICKENS

Goal: Find the fulfillment and joy that comes from pouring out your life for others.

Strategy: Determine creative ways to give generously using the time, talents, and resources you currently have.

In early 2012, my husband and I boarded a plane to visit the Dominican Republic. Neither of us had ever traveled outside the United States, let alone to a third-world country. There we would come face-to-face with poverty and lack. We were both out of our comfort zones—away from the familiar, from what we take for granted. Jesse and I knew this trip would be an eye-opening and heart-stirring adventure. We just didn't know exactly what to expect or how it would affect us in the long term.

This amazing opportunity came as a part of our financial commitment to Compassion International (CI), a Christian nonprofit organization that helps children who live in the poorest nations of the world. We were involved specifically with the Child Survival Program, which utilizes local churches to help save the lives of babies and mothers in poverty. Donations help fund prenatal and health care, nutritious foods and supplements, spiritual guidance and support, and infant training for mothers as well as medical and other care for their babies.[1] Going to the Dominican Republic gave us the chance to witness firsthand the lives of those we were able to help in some way.

Over a four-day period, Jesse and I experienced sights, smells, and tastes we were unaccustomed to in our everyday lives. We walked through a makeshift village located next to a large landfill where families survived on the scraps they carefully dug out. We hugged and played with children who slept on dirt floors with their entire families, piled like sardines on top of one dingy mattress. We cried and prayed with a sixteen-year-old mother of two, housed in a dilapidated hut without plumbing or electricity. We ate food that we weren't sure what it was or how it was cooked.

During our trip, we experienced a wide range of emotions. We fell in love with beautiful children and were broken by the filth and stench in which they were forced to live. We were disheartened by the immense struggle of moms, young and old alike, simply to survive; yet our hearts soared at the hope we saw in their eyes at being given the opportunity through CI to get out of poverty and live a better life.

I expected to have a lot of mixed feelings on the trip, so the heartache and hope packed into each day didn't come as a surprise. What I didn't expect to feel, however, was inspired and excited. Instead of coming home completely overwhelmed by the needs of the poverty-stricken, I felt invigorated by the opportunities to help.

I realized our little family could make a huge difference in the lives of others by living frugally and managing our resources well. For years, we had lived on a budget and sought to manage our money well, mostly so that we could avoid the stress and strain that often is a counterpart to carrying debt. We had set big financial goals for our family, but we had never set big giving goals. Yes, we had always given to our local church and to others in need, as we were able, but until visiting the Dominican Republic we never realized just how much financial stewardship and giving are intertwined.

All of a sudden, sticking with a budget wasn't just about us; it was about others. Through this humbling experience, we found the ultimate heartbeat for our finances—living simply so we can give generously. The more we save, the more we have to give. I came home with so much more passion, purpose, and motivation for clipping coupons, shopping sales, buying used goods, saving more, and spending less.

LOOK BEYOND YOURSELF

A big part of living with intention is to give and do for others. Our lives are not just about us and how we can manage our time, organize our priorities, and live each day with passion and purpose. It's also about looking for a need and finding a way to fill it.

It doesn't require much effort to find avenues, simple or creative, to help others. Take a look around your neighborhood, church, community, or social and professional networks. It won't take long to find a struggling individual or family you can serve in some way. You can do this by donating your time, your money, or even your natural abilities and talents. We all have something we can give, even if it's just a cup of cold water to someone on a hot day.

> Many small people, in many small places, do many small things that can alter the face of the world.
> —ANONYMOUS

I'D LIKE TO HELP, BUT . . .

Most of us want to give but are faced with certain challenges that make it seem impractical. It's natural for sacrificial giving to get taken down a notch or two on our priority lists. Maybe your finances are limited, you're a new (and exhausted) mom, or between your job, the kids, going to school, taking care of an aging parent, and life in general, you just can't find the time.

True, there are certain seasons in your life when you won't be able to give of your time, services, or money to the extent you'd like. Don't feel badly about it. Do what you can. If it's not much at this point in time, it's okay.

As I interact with women, I hear about common obstacles that keep us from giving our time, talents, and treasure to help those who are struggling. Maybe you can't donate a few hundred dollars to provide clean water in a third-world country or volunteer at a homeless shelter ten hours a week, but there are ways you can bring hope to those in your community and around the world.

Remember, there's no competition when it comes to giving. What matters most is your heart. Give what you can, even if it's a few dollars, an hour, or just a smile! If we each do what we can, collectively, we can make a huge difference in the world as we know it.

> We make a living by what we get. We make a life by what we give.
> —WINSTON CHURCHILL

I've Got No Money

I remember back when Jesse and I were newly married and money was tight. Though times were rough, I had so much fun trying to stretch our minimal thirty-dollars-per-week grocery budget as far as possible. It might seem weird that I'd call it fun, but I knew I had a choice: I could fret and mope about our tight budget or look at it as a challenge to be conquered. So I chose to approach our finances with a can-do, creative attitude.

I employed a variety of tactics to do this. I planned menus based on what was on sale, looked for marked-down produce and meat, stuck with inexpensive meals, and used coupons. By pairing coupons with rock-bottom sales and rebates, I often got household items we regularly used like canned goods, food staples, toiletries, and cleaning products for really cheap—or even free. Sometimes I even made a few extra bucks!

While I didn't have any money to donate, I could donate my

time and effort to find great deals and get free products, many of which were essentials that most people use on a regular basis. If I knew of someone in my church or community who was struggling financially, I'd ask them what items they use every day and collect a bag of those things from my stockpile closet. Maybe I couldn't give them money to cover their rent, but I could make sure they had plenty of soap, laundry detergent, toothpaste, and toilet paper!

There were other ways I helped people that didn't require money. I babysat for a friend for free so she and her husband could go out to dinner. I wrote cards and e-mails of encouragement. I prayed for people who were struggling. We opened our home to guests. I made meals for a family who had a child diagnosed with cancer. None of these things required a ton of effort or exploded our lives beyond repair. In fact, my deeds often felt pretty meager. But sometimes it's the little things that matter most.

Even when my husband and I were pinching pennies, we were still able to find ways to give to others. We've been so blessed in stepping out and giving, no matter how big or small the sacrifice. And we've learned that the more you freely and generously give, the more you receive—not necessarily always in the form of financial blessings, but in many other ways. Truly, "it is more blessed to give than to receive" (Acts 20:35).

> No one has ever become poor by giving.
> —ANNE FRANK

I Don't Have Time

If something is important enough to you, you'll make time

for it. However, even if your plate is full right now, that doesn't mean you can't still live a life with outstretched arms—even in little ways. Just like giving doesn't have to take a lot of money, it also doesn't have to take a lot of time. It can be as little as giving a hug or a smile, or sending someone a quick text or e-mail to tell her you're praying for or appreciate her.

In addition, consider how you can make giving a part of your everyday life. If you're making meat loaf for dinner, double the recipe and take the extra pan to a neighbor who just had a new baby. If you're headed to the store, call your friend who is sick and see if you can pick up any groceries for her.

I Have Young Kids and No Childcare

There are so many ways to give, even when you are busy caring for young children. The easiest way to juggle giving when you have little ones is not to make it a juggling act. Instead, involve your kids. Here are a few ideas:

- Have them help you bake cookies for a shut-in.
- Make cards together for someone who is in the hospital.
- Run a lemonade stand to collect money to donate to a local food pantry or other charitable organization.
- Collect toys for kids during Christmas.
- Visit nursing homes and have them play simple games with the residents.
- Invite widows into your home for lunch or a tea party.

Adrienne, a blog reader, shared the following story with me recently of how she was able to make a difference with her young daughter.

I am a firm believer that you should always help with a need when you can. But when my husband was in his last year of school, we hardly had enough of anything to help ourselves, let alone anyone else. I knew there had to be some way I could still make the lives of those who were struggling a little easier and show them that they were not forgotten. I just had to get creative about it.

For some reason, seeing homeless people on the side of the road has always pulled hard on my heartstrings. It's difficult for me to imagine living like that, to have nothing and no one at all. My children must have inherited that same compassion, as they are always willing to give out money to those in need. Except, in this particular season of our lives, we had none to give.

As part of keeping a tight budget, I taught myself to coupon. After a while, I had more toothpaste, shampoo, conditioner, floss, soap, cleansers, lotions, etc., than I would ever use. My daughter and I decided to put those samples to good use and make little "care packs" to pass out to the homeless people we saw on the side of the road.

We made a goal to fill ten care packs; once we had given them all away, we would make more. We purchased brown paper lunch sacks, which my daughter colored with Bible verses and pictures, and filled them with samples we accumulated along with some water bottles, canned soup, and plastic spoons we found on sale. Due to the particular type of samples, some of the care packs were geared more toward one gender so we marked the bags accordingly.

One day as we were on our way out to run errands, I told

my daughter to grab two bags to take with us. Unbeknownst to me, she had brought one female and one male care pack instead of two gender-neutral ones. I said a silent prayer as we drove around that we would find a male and female we could bless. Not long after, as we pulled up to a red light, a couple walked up to our car. My little girl was ecstatic as she handed them the two packs. The smile on her face was priceless!

In the big picture, this might seem like such a small act of kindness, but in making the effort, I was able to reach beyond my own financial situation, help someone else, and teach my daughter (and myself) how important it is to bless others . . . no matter what our circumstances may be.

I Don't Know Where to Start

There are people in need everywhere. You just have to look around and pay attention. Notice the elderly lady down the street who lives alone. Or the mother who just lost her husband to cancer. Or the boy in your child's class who has been sick for a long time. Or the neighbor who was injured in a car accident.

Start simple. Make a list of two or three people you know who are going through a hard time. Then think of something you can do for each person (like sending a card, e-mailing with a specific offer to help, baking a batch of cookies, or even giving them an anonymous small gift of cash or a gift card). Once you've made this list, make a commitment to carry out your ideas within the next two weeks. Put it on your calendar and then do it.

If you are intentional about doing one project like this each week, giving to others will start becoming second nature to you.

CREATIVE WAYS TO HELP OTHERS

There are many ways we can help others that don't require a lot of preparation or money. Here are some suggestions to get the wheels turning in your brain:

- Instead of going out for dinner with your girlfriends, plan a night in. Cook a few freezer meals together for a local family in need and bring them over the next day.
- Research your community for ways to volunteer (e.g., a senior center, the library, a nursing home, a soup kitchen).
- Plan a weekly or monthly family night out, and spend a few hours volunteering with your family at a church or other charitable organization.
- If you know someone who is pinching pennies, donate your coupons to them.
- Organize a clothing drive among your friends and loved ones, and donate those items to a local shelter.
- Make a weekly meal or two for an elderly neighbor.
- Help out a single mom by cleaning her house or watering her garden.
- Donate your childcare services to a tired new mom.
- Walk someone's dog for him or her.
- Teach someone a skill (like computers, a new language, or reading).
- If you travel frequently, save up travel-size toiletries and donate them to a local food pantry or homeless shelter.
- Write a handwritten note to encourage someone going through a difficult time.

- Visit the parking lot of a grocery store and return shopping carts where they belong.
- Help load someone's groceries into his or her car.
- Feed parking meters with spare change you find in your car or house.
- Bake some cookies or treats for your local civil servants like police officers and firefighters.
- Deliver handwritten notes to residents of senior living facilities.
- Remember the care packs that Adrienne handed out to homeless people? You can do the same thing. Just fill paper sacks or gallon-size Ziploc bags with toiletries.

THE REWARDS OF GIVING

When a publisher contacted me in late 2010 to offer me a book deal, I was hesitant to accept it. The thought of being a published author was exciting, but I was scared. Scared of the work involved. Scared of the looming deadline. Scared of the strain it might put on my health, my marriage, and our family.

But the biggest reason I was uncomfortable about publishing a book was the money issue. We didn't need the money. Sure, I could have come up with a savings goal we could put it toward, but it just didn't feel right. Besides, it seemed weird to expect people to buy a book about saving money when they probably didn't have much to begin with.

I was washing dishes one day and wrestling with what to do about the offer when I felt God speak to me in my heart: *Give it all away, Crystal. Take the book deal, but give away all your proceeds.*

Without a doubt, I knew that's what I was supposed to do. I also instinctively knew that I wanted to give all the proceeds of my book to Compassion International's Child Survival Program.

For the first time since I'd gotten the book offer, I felt excited about it. This project was no longer about me. It was no longer just about writing a book. It was about something much bigger. It was a channel for me to help meet the basic needs of those who were impoverished.

So I accepted the offer and spent the first half of 2011 writing and editing my first book. It was a lot of work. I often had to ask God to give me strength and wisdom beyond what I humanly possessed in order to pull off this massive endeavor. But through it all, I felt an overwhelming sense of peace and purpose. I was excited to think that this book wasn't going to just help thousands of lives in America. It would also influence many more lives through the money it raised for CI. That exhilarating thought kept me going even when I was tired and drained.

It's an indescribable feeling to invest your life in something that is much bigger than yourself. It's humbling and rewarding beyond measure. And being able to visit the Child Survival Program site in the Dominican Republic the following year and meet those wonderful women and children face-to-face took my gratitude to a whole new level. Seeing their lives changed for the better through the organization's efforts made all the hard work worth it.

THE DIFFERENCE ONE CAN MAKE

Carrie, one of my blog readers, wrote a beautiful post about how she was able to serve the children in her local community. I hope her words and story inspire you as they did me.

Three years ago, our forty-member church started giving away backpacks and school supplies every August for children in our area. I secured a list of families who were struggling financially and began collecting donations from stores like Target and Meijer, as well as from individuals. These donations were used to fill backpacks for 150 kids. To top it off, with the help of a local salon, we also offered free back-to-school haircuts. It was incredible!

Fast-forward three years, to this past August. So many backpacks and supplies were donated that we had a bunch left over. I called two local schools and asked them if they could use those items. One individual told me they could use the backpacks to send food home to children who needed it. I was astonished, heartbroken, and saddened to hear that there were children in our area who didn't have enough to eat.

Since this particular school already had a food program in place, I had an idea for the other school that was taking the remainder of our backpacks. I told them that we wanted to provide food for children who needed it via a backpack each week. The school loved our idea and sent home surveys to get a feel for how many could use the help.

The response was overwhelming. Parents signed up eighteen children to participate. Every Friday we filled backpacks with seven meals they could eat over the weekend (including items like canned goods, juice boxes, shelf-stable milk, macaroni and cheese, granola bars, and cereal). Our little church, providing food that cost us less than ten dollars for each child, was able to make a big difference in a small way. What an amazing feeling!

A few months later I discovered a national organization called Blessings in a Backpack that does the same thing in a more official capacity. If you're looking for an opportunity to serve or want to consider this program for your local school, check out their website, BlessingsinaBackpack.org.

I am so thankful to God that He has blessed us in a way that we can be a blessing to others!

> We often need to lose sight of our priorities in order to see them.
> —JOHN IRVING

A NEW PERSPECTIVE

When we are attuned to the great needs that exist in this world and help make a difference, something happens. It creates in us a shift in perspective. Instead of focusing on what we don't have, we begin to appreciate the countless blessings we do have. Instead of complaining, we become thankful. Instead of seeing obstacles in our lives, we recognize opportunities.

One morning, a few days after we arrived home from our trip to the Dominican Republic, I woke up and immediately knew something was wrong. My face felt hot and engorged, and I was having trouble opening my eyes. I ran into the bathroom to look in the mirror and check out what on earth was going on. I gasped when I saw my reflection. Half of my face was swollen, red, and painful. One of my eyes was almost swollen shut.

A washcloth soaked in ice-cold water did little to alleviate the swelling, and my skin began to severely itch. We decided I'd better get things checked out by the doctor. After examining me, she determined I'd had a severe allergic reaction. In time, the medication began to work and the swelling and pain went down.

Spending the morning at the doctor's office was inconvenient. Dealing with the pain and swelling for hours was uncomfortable. I cringed just looking at the unpleasant sight of my face in the mirror. I hoped I wouldn't see anyone I knew that morning. And I was worried about what my swollen face might look like in a few days when I was scheduled to speak at an event.

But truthfully, it was hard for me to stay stressed over my swollen face. Instead, I kept thinking of Laney, one of the Child Survival Program moms I had met in the Dominican Republic the week before.

Laney is a mother of three and lives in a fly-infested, dilapidated shack. Her home does have an outdoor toilet, a refrigerator, and a stove, but its flimsy construction provides little protection from the elements. And because it sits near a garbage dump, the stench mixed with the hot, humid air is just about unbearable.

But Laney didn't seem to mind her less-than-desirable residence. All she could talk about was how thankful she was to have a part-time job and three children. Laney's face beamed as she told me how grateful she also was to have a leg. I had trouble understanding what she was saying through the interpreter until she pulled up her pant leg. I was shocked to see that a large section of her ankle and calf was missing. I learned she had been in a motorcycle accident and had almost lost her entire leg.

I also noticed Laney's face had a large scar on it. I assumed this, too, was from the crash, but she told me it came from her abusive husband. He went in a rage one night and bit her. He left two months ago and she hadn't seen him since.

As I stood in front of the mirror at home looking at my swollen face, I stared at my reflection with a new perspective. Instead of being bothered by my appearance and discomfort, I focused on the many blessings I have—like money to visit a doctor, a husband who cares for me, good health, clean water, and access to medicine. The list is endless. A swollen face is really a drop in the ocean in light of the enormous burdens and difficulties of those around us and all over the world.

> Gratitude is not only the greatest of virtues, but the parent of all the others.
> —CICERO

PASS IT ON

One of my greatest hopes as a parent is that my three children will be givers. Jesse and I want our kids to really and truly understand that everything we have has been given to us by God and that our role is to be conduits of His blessings to others. Whether we have a little or a lot, the more we open our hands and hearts to others and give generously, the more we're blessed in return.

Think about what a great legacy you are leaving your children when you teach them how to make a difference in the lives of others. This is how you raise life changers.

Giving has been an important part of our home life, and my husband and I have sought to model a giving and serving lifestyle to our children. However, when kids are young, it's hard to know how much of what you are teaching them is really sinking in. But in the past few years, I've discovered maybe they were picking up more than I realized.

Our family was riding in the van one November day and Kathrynne (age six at the time) blurted out of nowhere, "Mom, I'd really like to do Operation Christmas Child boxes." (This program, sponsored by Samaritan's Purse, sends shoeboxes full of toys, toiletries, and other items to children in need all over the world.)

We had done them in the past, and I was already hoping we could do them again this year, so I said, "Sure, honey, we can definitely do that. Did you have anything specific in mind?"

"Well," she said, "I was thinking I could take the money that I've been saving all year to pay for them."

I sat up in my seat and looked back into her eyes. She was completely serious.

And then she said, "I'd like to do ten boxes. Five for girls and five for boys."

At this point, my husband and I both had tears in our eyes. You see, Kathrynne had been saving all year for a large-ticket item. She'd done a lot of chores to earn the money, and after tithing, we let her set aside the rest for this item she wanted to buy. She couldn't stop talking about it and was delighted because she had almost reached her savings goal. Yet she wanted to use almost all her hard-earned and carefully saved money to fill ten Operation Christmas Child boxes.

Over the course of the next week, Kathrynne made a list of what she wanted to buy. Then she shopped for toiletries, small toys, and crayons and paid for everything with her own money. Finally, she wrote cards to the children, helped pack the boxes, and took them with me to the drop-off point in town.

THE JOY OF A CHILD'S SACRIFICE

As a parent, I couldn't have been prouder of my child. And by the smile on Kathrynne's face and her uncontainable excitement, I knew providing for others was so much more fulfilling to her than buying that long-saved-for item ever would have been.

But I was more than just proud. I was deeply touched and challenged to examine my own heart and attitude toward giving. I realized that while I love to give to others, often I'll give from my abundance instead of giving in a way that costs me something near and dear.

Kathrynne didn't give from her abundance. She gave up buying something she had long waited for so she could help children who had little or nothing. It was worth it. Kathrynne knew there were others who needed the money more than she needed a new toy.

Instead of me teaching my daughter about giving, she's the one teaching me through her example. And I'm left inspired and motivated to give generously without worrying about what I might have to give up in return.

WHAT YOU WANT TO KNOW ▮▮▮▮▮▮ ▮▮▮▮▮▮ ▮▮▮▮

Q: How can I teach my children to become givers?

A: First and foremost, set an example before your children. You cannot expect them to be givers if you are not one yourself. Don't nag or rush your child to do kind things for others. Do them yourself first. Many times they will simply follow your lead.

Encourage your child to share his or her allowance. If you give your children money for chores, have them use a portion of their earnings to do something nice for someone else. For example, they can buy a small toy for a child in a hospital or save up that money to buy a larger item (like diapers, a coat, or other necessities) for a local shelter or other charitable organization.

Show your child the poverty and needs that exist all over the world. The point is not to frighten them but to open their eyes to a world beyond their own. Browse through websites of organizations like Compassion International that depict hunger and homelessness. Then do something to help, like sponsor a child.

Make a gift basket together for a local family in need. You can collect items like toiletries, cleaning products, food, and other necessities. Have them wrap each item or the entire package on their own.

Give your child a gift card to use to buy gifts for a cause. My friend JessieLeigh shared this idea with me. She says, "Children have amazingly giving spirits. They also love to get to choose things and to be 'in charge.' To help instill a giving attitude in your children, give them a ten- or twenty-dollar gift card to a local supermarket for Christmas or their birthdays and let them choose canned goods for a local food pantry. The adventure of getting to shop is as good as a new toy for many little ones!" This could also be a great way to learn some practical math lessons to boot.

Another option is to click and give. Even if you don't have any money to donate, you can visit TheHungerSite .com. A click of a mouse will prompt a sponsor to donate cups of food to those in need.

Remember, giving is a lifestyle. Don't just show compassion on holidays or special occasions. Make it something that you do all year round.

BE GENEROUS WITH YOURSELF

My friend Laura is a mom of three who just oozes generosity in her life. The first time I met her, I was immediately drawn to her beautiful smile and sweet spirit. She's also an amazing writer who has repeatedly challenged me through her words.

Not too long ago, she wrote and shared about a movie she'd watched. One of the characters in the movie said something about "being generous with yourself" and that phrase stuck with her and caused her to step back and examine her own life. In Laura's beautiful fashion, she inspired me to realize that the greatest gift we can give to others is ourselves. She gave me permission to share the following from what she wrote:

Lately, I've been considering how I can be more generous with myself to my family—especially my children. Too often, I feel the tendency to wallow in self-pity. My broken record drones, "I am now a servant who had to sacrifice her colorful personality to these people I love so much. I'm invisible. They don't understand. Nobody knows the real me." Blah, blah, blah. If I don't snap that broken record in half, I listen to it. And I close up with resentment. Life becomes very bland and arduous. My family misses the gift of me, and they are surprisingly sad and disconnected because of it.

As a mother I am a servant, but my job description is to dig deeply into how God has made me so that I can give my family me. I've been scheming about how I can live vibrantly and bring my family right along with me.

After reading this, I e-mailed Laura and asked her if I could interview her for this book, because her words had such a profound impact on me. Here's our conversation:

ME. What does "being generous with yourself" mean to you?

LAURA. I think it means acknowledging that God gave me a distinct personality, thoughts, and gifts so that I could bless other people and glorify Him. It means being the clay pot, happily used the way the Maker sees best. I got tired of being frightened and guarded, so I decided to trust God, be grateful for who I am, and offer more of my thoughts, enthusiasm, support, and love to other people.

ME. Why does this quote impact you so much?

LAURA. I have always felt compelled to live like Bob Dylan's famous song "Shelter from the Storm." You know, the woman who says, "Come in, I'll give you shelter from the storm." I've wanted to be the outstretched arms, the hopeful heart, and the kind words that others may need. My journals are packed with quotes and meditations on being hospitable, generous, and kind. Yet I've been too timid to embrace this lifestyle.

I don't struggle with giving my possessions, but I do struggle with trusting other people, sharing my thoughts, and loving people nonjudgmentally and without jealousy. I do struggle to believe that my friendship and support are beneficial to others. I do struggle in affirming and serving other people when the work is dirty, difficult, and frightening. So my whole journey to become gracious, hospitable, and kind is the Holy Spirit helping me say yes to the command Jesus gave to follow Him.

ME. What are some ways you've sought to be generous with yourself?

LAURA. I've given more of my genuine admiration, affection, and inner thought life to my husband, who loves every ounce of it. I've enjoyed the generosity that is demanded in motherhood—sharing my prayers, thoughts, and support with my children. I've grown as a friend to the amazing women God has placed in my life. I've worked on picking up the phone, e-mailing, and texting to check in on people I genuinely care about, but struggled to express my care and affection. My prayer life has grown as I've given my time to other people so much more that they invade my heart and I pray for them continually. I laugh more, cry more, offer my spiritual gifts more freely (and more often), don't wallow in jealousy, and don't wallow in insecurity nearly as much as I used to.

Laura has inspired me so much on my own journey. And I've since been looking for opportunities where I can give of myself as a result. I want to encourage you, too, to step outside your comfort zone. Give freely and generously of yourself, your resources, and your time. Live your life with arms outstretched.

I promise you'll be blessed beyond what you can imagine!

> Let us not be satisfied with just giving money. Money is not enough, money can be got, but they need your hearts to love them. So, spread your love everywhere you go.
>
> —MOTHER TERESA

GET PRACTICAL

There are countless ways to help others. You can give of your time, your resources, your skills, or your money to a worthy cause, family, or individual. Take some time and think of three ways you can give to others this month. Start by paying attention to the needs in your local community. Who can you help down the block, down the road, or across town?

Take this challenge a step further, and think of what you can give that might take you out of your comfort zone. Maybe donate a portion of or all the money you've been saving for something special to a worthy charity instead. Or give up a spa treatment and use that time to spend with an elderly neighbor. You might even consider using your vacation days to go on a mission trip for a few days or a week.

Make a note to write or talk about your experience afterward. How did it make you feel? What did you learn in the process? How were you blessed? Share your story with others.

9

Sometimes It *Is* About You

When the well's dry, we know the worth of water.
—BENJAMIN FRANKLIN

Goal: Feel more refreshed and rested in order to face life with passion and gusto.

Strategy: Be intentional about carving out time to recharge through plugging in to relationships that will energize you, taking time to nurture yourself, and making your health and well-being a priority.

I was having one of those days.

I was tired and not feeling well. Our family was in the middle of last-minute Christmas preparations. I was in the thick of marketing and publicity for my first book. And because my assistant was out of town, I was juggling a lot of extra tasks on my plate.

I went downstairs to get something out of the basement and noticed the floor was sopping wet. The closer I got to the utility room, the more I knew something was very wrong.

I opened the door and my mouth dropped open. Two inches of water covered the entire floor, and more water was gushing out of the sump pump.

Truthfully, I wanted to go back upstairs and cry. I was overwhelmed at the thought of how much work the cleanup was going to take—and my plate was already full! But instead of wallowing in self-pity, I called my kids downstairs and we started mopping up the water as quickly as we could.

The more we cleaned, mopped, and bailed out water, the more I realized just how much had seeped in to almost our entire basement. Having exhausted our efforts, I called my husband at work and asked him to come home. After assessing the situation, we decided to call a company who specializes in water damage to help clean up.

I thought the job might run us a few hundred dollars. I wasn't thrilled about spending the extra money, but it was definitely worth it. Especially if we were able to salvage all the carpet, padding, baseboards, and walls from getting ruined.

I was a bit naive.

The repair crew came out within a few hours and estimated that it would cost us more than six thousand dollars to fix. What? I had to look at the number multiple times just to make sure I wasn't accidentally seeing an extra zero. The price was well beyond what we had in our budget, so we opted to do the job ourselves. We borrowed fans and dehumidifiers from neighbors, asked a friend to help us move our furniture and pull up the carpet, and labored as a family to dry our basement. It was a huge headache and took hours of time.

What was most frustrating was that this problem could have been easily prevented. You see, we'd been having problems with our sump pump a few weeks before. It was making a weird grinding noise, wouldn't turn off, and started smelling like it was burning. I was scared the pump was going to explode or catch fire, so I unplugged it. I meant to tell Jesse that evening and have him look at it but, well, life happened and I completely forgot.

As long as there wasn't any rain, there was no problem. But when the rain came, our basement started flooding. Without an activated and working sump pump, it was bound to happen. While I still kick myself over my irresponsibility, looking back I realize what a perfect analogy this is to our own lives.

So much of the time, our exhaustion and burnout are the result of not being plugged in. We think we're capable of handling life without constantly renewing our power supplies. It might work out fine so long as life is sailing smoothly. But when the rains of stress, change, sickness, or upheaval come pouring down upon us, we quickly start drowning.

Here's the deal. We can't survive the storms of life without regularly taking care of ourselves. It's too much. Oh, we might be able to hold it together for a little while, slapping on our happy faces and pretending that everything's okay, but we won't be able to keep up the facade for long.

I know, because that was me, remember? I was unplugged and heading to total burnout.

BURNOUT—IT HAPPENS

Whether you're a stay-at-home mom, work outside the house, don't have children, are climbing the career ladder, or whatever your situation—if you feel overwhelmed, tired, stressed, and stretched to the max, burnout is a legitimate threat. I don't want to be a Debbie Downer, but I'll even go so far to say it's inevitable at some point. If there's no relief in sight from stress and exhaustion, especially without ongoing self-care, any normal human being is bound to break. While burnout is no fun, it happens. And more often and to more people than you can imagine.

Through my own experience and in speaking to thousands of women across the country, I've learned that we need to take better care of ourselves. Instinctively, we want to take care of everything and everyone around us, but in the process we forget to look inward and help ourselves.

When you start taking steps to live your life on purpose—saying yes only to the best, setting boundaries and saying no more often, being conscious of how you spend your time and money—you run less of a risk of breaking down. But if you're slogging it out in survival mode and need ways to regroup mentally, emotionally, or even spiritually, I have some suggestions.

Self-care looks different for everyone. Some women need more sleep than others. Some women de-stress through exercise. Others benefit more from a few hours of quiet reading or having coffee with a friend. However, there are some basic tips that would benefit any woman and help her recharge her internal batteries.

> We can be tired, weary and emotionally distraught, but after spending time alone with God, we find that He injects into our bodies energy, power and strength.
> —CHARLES STANLEY

Because my schedule is quite full and I've shouldered the crushing weight that comes from not being regularly charged, I've found it's important to plug in relationally—with God, my spouse, and others.

PLUG IN TO GOD AND HIS WORD

As a Christian, I believe wholeheartedly that I can't do this mothering thing on my own. In fact, I can't do life on my own—period. I desperately need God each step of the way. In John 7:37–38, Jesus says, "If anyone thirsts, let him come to me and drink. Whoever believes in me, as the Scripture has said, 'Out of his heart will flow rivers of living water.'"

Don't look to other people, books, diets, programs, pills, or even a church to give you the strength you need to live the life God has called you to live. All those resources can be helpful, but they can never give you what you will find in Christ alone.

I encourage you to get regular spiritual refreshment by praying and reading the Bible every day. Keep it simple. Spending time with God doesn't require an elaborate, complicated plan. For instance, I like to pray while I'm running on the treadmill.

Also, spend time with God's Word. Again, keep things simple. Don't set yourself up for failure by trying to have a two-hour Bible-reading session every morning. The point is not the amount of time it takes but that you are soaking up wisdom and strength from God's Word.

I love what Rachael Jankovic says in her book *Loving the Little Years*: "The state of your heart is the state of your home."[1] You have to feed your soul before you can be a great leader, owner of a company, daughter, sister, wife, friend, boss, manager, or mother. You may think you do not have time to feed yourself spiritually, but I assure you that you cannot afford not to.

PLUG IN TO YOUR MARRIAGE

If you are married, your relationship with your spouse must be your next priority. It's easy to say, of course, but much harder to live out. This is an area in my life where I've faltered and struggled over the years. There have been times when my husband has been shortchanged because I've gotten my priorities out of whack and allowed other things to consume me.

By the grace of God, I've made some big changes in the past few years to show Jesse how important he is to me. What has helped me tremendously is to regularly ask him if he feels significant. If you've not done this in a while (or ever), I highly recommend it if you're feeling brave and braced for the answer. Ask your spouse what specifically you can do to make him feel like he is your top priority. You might be surprised at his answer. I know I was!

Jesse once told me he'd rather come home to a messy house, a makeup-free wife in sweats, and a peanut butter and jelly dinner as long as I was cheerful and happy to see him and spend time with him. Since I express love by doing and I'm very much a type A, check-things-off-my-to-do-list type of gal, this has been hard for me. But just sitting and being together with him is what my husband loves best. And you know what? When I plug in to our relationship in this way, I always end up having a great time and feeling loved myself.

Commit to keeping the friendship and romance alive in your marriage. You'll quickly find out how a solid, energizing marriage will revitalize you from the inside out.

PLUG IN TO FRIENDSHIPS

For a long time, I didn't have any close friends other than my husband. Though I went to church and was involved in our community, in my heart I felt so alone. I wasn't alone because people didn't try to get close to me, but because I wouldn't let them.

I'd been wounded and rejected in the past by others, so I was afraid to trust or open up to anyone. I was afraid to be vulnerable. I was afraid to get hurt again. And I was afraid to just be me, assuming that no one would like the real me if they got to know me well.

One day I was reading a blog post by Ann Voskamp, and something she wrote hit me like a ton of bricks: "No one tells you that the shields you carry to keep you safe, they become the steel cages that keep you alone."[2] I felt she was speaking right to me.

The protective wall I had built around me made me feel safe—and very lonely. I realized there was only one way I was ever going to build the close friendships I longed for. I had to be willing to put myself out there and be honest, authentic, and vulnerable with others. To do so meant I was risking getting hurt again, but it was a risk I was willing to take.

I started praying that God would give me a few friends I could trust and with whom I felt safe. I'm an introvert by nature and prefer deep relationships versus surface ones. I began looking at my circle of acquaintances and reaching out to women I wanted to connect with on a deeper level.

At first, it was really hard. Doubts circled my mind like vultures. *What if they don't like me? What if they think my idea for getting together is dumb?* I pushed through those fears, however, and continued to reach out. Not every invitation for coffee turned into a close friendship (and that was okay). But through those efforts some beautifully rich, authentic friendships were created.

You may be in the same boat I was, needing friendships but fearing rejection or hurt. Here are some suggestions.

Cultivate What You Already Have

Instead of thinking that the grass will be greener if you move, change churches, or join a different moms group, start with the networks that already surround you. Look within your office, Bible study, social/ministry/volunteer groups you're a part of, or places you regularly frequent (like the gym or park), and find a woman or two with whom you could see yourself developing a close friendship.

Take the First Step

Don't wait for someone to invite you over for dinner or out to coffee. Take initiative and extend the invitation first.

Be Honest

If you want to build an authentic friendship, you've got to be open and honest. This doesn't mean you need to air all your dirty laundry or share absolutely every facet of your life or self. But you do have to be real. Don't pretend you're someone you're not. Don't hide behind false pretenses. Be you!

WHY REST MATTERS

A dear woman I've met through blogging, Arabah, recently explained how she managed to get through a difficult time period in her life. Due to a plethora of high-stress changes within a short amount of time, she succumbed to burnout. Here is how she coped and found her way back to a more restful place.

A few years ago, our family went through a period of adjustment unlike any other. We adopted, moved internationally that same month, changed ministry roles, and had three children in less than two years. Trying to keep up with all the changes and demands was more than I had time for! Although I am accustomed to living a high-octane life due to the nature of our work, this time I did not spring back like normal. I was overwhelmed and burned out and had no idea what to do.

When my youngest was born, it was the straw that broke the camel's back. I was emotionally, physically, and spiritually drained. I knew that in order to be healthy and have a healthy home life, I had to be intentional about making some changes. I also knew I had a huge obstacle to overcome: accepting that margin and rest were really okay.

I had the idea that I was somehow not doing my job if I took regular time-outs. And then there were the logistics of how it was all to be worked out that threatened to make me give up. Then I realized that Jesus Himself frequently withdrew to a quiet place. Even He needed time to be alone and refresh internally. With His example in mind, I began to make my changes, which included:

Observing a weekly Sabbath rest (not necessarily on Sunday). This is one day a week where I have nothing scheduled and we all stay at home as a family.

Eating healthfully. For a time, this included having someone come to our house to cook dinner five times a week. (Don't hate me for that one!)

Going to bed early so I can get up an hour or so before the kids wake up. I use this morning alone time to be spiritually renewed.

Exercise, an investment with huge dividends. I strive to exercise five times a week.

A daily routine. Having a schedule is too rigid for the life we live, so I use a routine instead. I jot down five things I want to accomplish each day and the order I need to do them in. This one little strategy has helped me tremendously. It ensures I am getting the important tasks done and that keeps my mind clear and unburdened. It also keeps my to-do list from getting out of hand.

MAKE TIME FOR YOU

One of the most important relationships you need to nurture is with yourself. Being self-focused isn't about being selfish or self-absorbed. In fact, many times when you direct your attention toward yourself and practice self-care, you become a better person all around. You transform into a more energetic mom, a more attentive spouse, a more tuned-in friend. You lead with more inspiration. You engage in life with more motivation and passion.

I've learned that when I focus on my health, read more, schedule time for fun, and give myself some grace, I become more the woman, wife, mother, and writer God has created me to be, instead of a stressed-out, frazzled mess. Let's unpack these practices.

> Health is certainly more valuable than money because it is by health that money is procured.
> —SAMUEL JOHNSON

FOCUS ON YOUR HEALTH

Taking care of your health should be a top priority. Just ask anyone who suffers from chronic pain or a debilitating disease. They know how important good health is because they battle with pain and sickness every day. When you go through a health setback, everything else falls to the wayside. All the things you thought were once important seem meaningless, and you would give anything to be healthy again.

If you're in relatively good health, why wouldn't you regularly practice good health habits? You can't afford not to. When we take care of our bodies, we actually experience less stress. Make better lifestyle choices, and you'll also be better equipped to prevent diseases like diabetes and high blood pressure. You'll feel better. You'll be less drained and more strengthened.

Now, you don't have to turn into a health nut who spends hours at the gym and stares at pastries through a glass window. I've incorporated some simple steps to improve my health that have made a significant difference. (And believe me, I like to have my chocolate.)

Eat Better

Food is your body's fuel. If you're mostly fueling yourself with doughnuts, candy bars, and soda, that's probably why you feel sluggish and rundown.

I recently read *Energy Explosion* by Arabah Joy (who talked about the importance of rest a little earlier).[3] She encourages us to start each meal with protein and produce. Fill up on fresh fruits, veggies, and protein before eating sugars, fats, and carbs. This will not only give you more energy, but it will also help you shed any unwanted pounds you're carrying around.

I've found it helpful to make raw fruits and veggies readily accessible. If I have a fridge full of bags of prewashed carrot sticks, cut-up fresh fruit, and hard-boiled eggs, I don't have an excuse for not eating healthy.

There's a balance, of course. It's completely okay to have some breads and sweets every once in a while, but make sure that your diet is primarily made up of protein, fruits, and veggies. I find it helpful to track what I eat on SparkPeople.com to make sure I'm eating a balanced diet.

Take Vitamins

I used to think you should get all the nutrition your body needs from food alone. While that may be possible for some people who live on a strict, regimented diet, the rest of us need a little extra boost. Years ago my husband encouraged me to start taking a high-quality multivitamin (I take Optimum Nutrition Opti-Women). I've been amazed at the difference that I've felt in my health and energy levels.

Try it. Take a high-quality multivitamin for three months and see if you feel any better. If you don't, at least you're not hurting yourself by consuming some extra vitamins and minerals.

I also recommend scheduling an appointment with your doctor to have routine blood work done. This will determine whether you have any vitamin, mineral, or nutrient deficiencies. If you struggle with low energy, it's possible you might be anemic or have other medical issues that can be easily and quickly remedied.

TIME TO SEEK PROFESSIONAL HELP

When I was deep in the midst of postpartum depression, I became a shell of myself. I barely functioned most days and had to force myself to get up in the morning, get dressed, and do the basic things I had to do to take care of my home and family. I had completely lost my zest for life. There was nothing I wanted to do, nowhere I wanted to go, and no one I wanted to talk to.

Things finally got so bad that I was willing to admit this was a battle I could not fight on my own. And with the help of my wonderful husband, wise professionals, much research, and friends who had been where I was, I embarked on the road to recovery. It took time, but eventually my vivacious and vibrant self came back. The dark clouds that once threatened to suffocate me dissipated. The sun started shining again.

I remember during this difficult time getting advice from someone to try to do something fun every day. Suffering from something as serious as PPD made me incapable of doing that. Following a simple plan of three steps or pulling myself up by my bootstraps wasn't going to change how severely depressed I was. That was a warning sign that I needed to get help—and quickly.

If you think you have something more than just the blues, please don't hide it. Reach out for help. You need the support of family, friends, and professionals to help you pull through. Like I was, you may be suffering from something more than physical exhaustion or fatigue. Make an appointment to see your doctor immediately. Don't be embarrassed about how you feel. Depression is common and treatable. Talk to your loved ones and seek help.

Drink More Water

If you are not drinking at least sixty-four ounces of water each day, you are not drinking enough. There are many benefits that can be reaped from regularly drinking that amount of water. Of course, change doesn't happen overnight. You have to be consistent with your water intake over a long period of time. And if you do . . .

- You'll be less dehydrated and have more energy.
- You can lower your risk of a heart attack.
- You'll retain less water (see you later, bloat!).
- Your skin will look better.
- Your digestive system will improve (goodbye, constipation!).
- You'll have less of a chance of getting colon cancer.
- You'll flush out and eliminate toxins from your body.

I always have a glass of water nearby, no matter where I am, and I never leave the house without a big water bottle.

Exercise

You don't have to spend hours at the gym (unless you want to and have the time). Even as little as a few minutes here and there during the day a few times a week can help.

Studies from the *American Journal of Sports Medicine* and *Preventive Medicine* show that frequent bouts of exercise yield plenty of health benefits.[4] For instance, short walks after dinner help reduce the amount of fat and triglyceride levels in the bloodstream. Spurts of activity throughout the day help to lower blood pressure and take inches off our bodies.

Exercise doesn't have to be complicated or take long. Just adding physical activity into your day helps. Move more. Get off the couch and do something for thirty minutes a few times a week. Walk around your neighborhood in the morning or evening. Play in the park with your kids or have a dance-a-thon with them. Pick up a sport and join a local team. Look into some classes at your community recreation center. Pop in an exercise DVD or follow fitness videos on YouTube. If you want to join a gym and work out for an hour a few times a week, great! Just know that any physical activity you do consistently is benefiting you.

There are a thousand excuses for why you can't or don't exercise, but I'm not buying any of them. Everyone can find at least ten minutes a few times per week to do something physical. Make exercise a priority. You are worth it.

Here are some fitness and nutrition resources that will equip you for better health:

- *Jillian Michael's 30-Day Shred.* You might not be able to walk without pain for a few days, but Jillian knows how to bring it! This is my favorite DVD of hers.
- Leslie Sansone's *Walk Away the Pounds.* This is a great low-impact exercise DVD to get your heart pumping. Your library should have at least a few of her DVDs.
- Tony Horton's P90X DVD series. For those of you looking for a hardcore, at-home fitness-training program, this is it. I've tried it. It's tough, but it works!
- Apps: Nike+, RunTracker, SparkPeople, MyFitnessPal

Sleep

I've said it before and I'll say it again—but without the lengthy explanation. Be sure you are getting the amount of zzz's your body and mind need to function properly and efficiently during the day.

> Take rest; a field that has rested gives a bountiful crop.
> —OVID

READ MORE

Reading a book may seem like a luxury, but it's important enough for me to include as part of my lifestyle. Why? It's simple. Reading challenges, inspires, shapes, and educates me. I wouldn't be the person I am today were it not for the meaningful and challenging books I've read over the course of my life. They help motivate me as a wife, mother, friend, business-woman, writer, and thinker.

A good book can open up a world to you that you might never experience yourself. Reading biographies about single moms and parents of children with disabilities or long-term illnesses helps me have a deeper understanding of their struggles and trials so I can better reach out to them. Reading books about different cultures and time periods has given me a better grasp on history and an appreciation of the modern conveniences and freedoms we have that many others did not and do not have. If you need a few suggestions, I've included a list of some of my favorite reads in the Recommended Resources section at the back of this book.

Pick up titles that have to do with your life priorities and your best stuff. If you're focused on your family, read books that center on being a positive influence in your home or raising your children in a godly manner. If one of your priorities has to do with making a difference in this world in a big way, look for books that will help you be a life changer. If improving your finances is at the top of your checklist, commit to reading topics about making wise financial decisions and investments.

WHAT YOU WANT TO KNOW

Q: I've been inspired by you to read more, but I'm struggling to find time to add reading to my day. How do you fit reading into your day?

A: Since I love to read and find so much benefit from reading, I'm always on a mission to fit more reading into my day. Here are a few things that I've found work well for me:

ALWAYS HAVE A BOOK HANDY

I keep a few books I'm working on reading through-out different parts of the house—one or two near my bed, one or two by the treadmill (I always read when I'm doing my warm-up and cool-down before and after running), and sometimes one or two on the kitchen countertop. That way, if I have a few minutes of extra time, I have a book handy to pick up and read. I always keep one in my purse to read if someone is driving me somewhere or if I'm waiting at the doctor's office or for any appointment. Sometimes I don't even get to crack it open. Other times I end up having unexpected waiting time and finishing the entire book.

READ FIRST THING IN THE MORNING

In the past few years, I've made reading a higher priority in my life as I feel it improves me as a writer and blogger. One way I've carved out more time is by read-ing first thing in the morning. On a typical morning, I get up early and spend twenty to thirty minutes reading the Bible and praying. As soon as I'm finished, instead of opening my laptop, I set the timer for ten minutes and read whatever book I'm into at the moment. I can usu-ally read at least a chapter in that short block of time. I've found it's a great way to start my day. Plus, if the day ends up being very full and there's no extra time for reading at any other time of the day, at least I've read one chapter of a book.

TURN OFF THE TV

If you usually spend an hour a day watching television, challenge yourself to read a book instead during that time—or at least for half of that time.

TURN OFF THE COMPUTER

The Internet is certainly a great tool for researching and finding information, but let's get real. How much time do you spend mindlessly browsing blogs or shopping sites and Googling random topics? Probably more time than you think. I admit. I used to waste time online. I've gotten sucked into the web to the point where it became noisy overload. I ended up really streamlining things a few years ago and now I follow a few blogs, visit a few sites, and use the extra time to do other more important things—like reading good books.

LISTEN TO AUDIOBOOKS

Are you in your car a lot? Do you have a long commute to work? Are you constantly driving your kids to this practice or that game? If snatching a few minutes of reading time seems beyond comprehension, consider audiobooks. You can listen to them anytime your hands are busy and your mind is free. My husband encouraged me to give audiobooks a try a few years ago, and I've truly enjoyed this extra way to fit in more reading.

I have a four-year-old, a two-year-old, and an almost three-month-old, with myself and my husband as the only caregivers/no babysitters. I'm realizing it is possible to read, even with little ones. Beyond having multiple books going at once, I also try to make sure I am reading at least one book in each of these three formats: paper, Kindle (on my iPhone), and audiobooks (also my iPhone) at any given time. I also try to read a variety of genres throughout the year.

—KEREN

SCHEDULE FUN

It's important to make time to do things that are fun, make you feel energized, and inspire you. Yes, I understand we all carry a load of responsibilities that take up our time, but when you're feeling stretched to the max, it's time to step back and ask yourself some questions: How much time are you spending doing things that drain you? How about doing things that energize you? If you've committed little to none of your time to enjoyment, you may have just found the solution to overcoming burnout.

First, jot down some things you love to do. Instead of thinking of your to-do lists, goals, and routines, clear your mind for ten or fifteen minutes and focus on the activities you enjoy. It can be anything such as reading a good book, getting a massage, spending time with close friends, cooking gourmet meals, writing poetry, running, dancing, painting, or scrapbooking. Think of things that excite you and make you feel alive, refreshed, and energized. Write them down.

Second, be intentional about scheduling in time for these activities. If you wrote down twenty things, I certainly don't expect you to spend time every day doing twenty things to relax or recharge. I want you to commit some time, maybe only an hour or two a week, to one or two activities that regularly replenish your energy stores.

Not only does this give you something to look forward to every week, but it also prevents you from wearing yourself too thin and becoming worn out. If you are regularly doing something that recharges you, you may be able to avoid burnout.

> I'm a stay-at-home mom of three kids and I also own a part-time home business. I've had many burnout moments over the years. It helps to get out of the house and do something fun like see a movie, watch a basketball game, or go to the bookstore. Getting a break from my daily routine keeps me energized.
>
> —CARA

One thing that has helped me prevent burnout is spending time alone, away from the noise and hustle and bustle of everyday life. While I love being with other people, I'm most refreshed with quiet. Almost every week I visit a coffee shop to write for a few hours, curl up in bed with a good book on Sunday afternoon, or go grocery shopping on my own. The stillness reenergizes me and makes me much more productive and passionate about life.

NEED MORE IDEAS TO RECHARGE?

If you're struggling to find ways to care for yourself, here are some simple ideas that may work for you:

- Unplug for a day or two. Turn off your cellphone and computer. Enjoy the quiet.
- Go to the gym and try a new class.
- Get a change of scenery. Visit your local park or someplace scenic where you can admire the view and simply breathe.
- Take a luxurious bubble bath (and read a good book while you're there).
- Go to a concert.
- Have a night out with your girlfriends.
- Start a gratitude journal and every day write down something you are thankful for.
- Do something fun with your husband, like take dance lessons.
- Plant a garden.
- Take a nap.
- Get some art supplies (raid your kids' rooms) and draw/color/paint something.
- Did I mention sleep?
- Splurge on a spa treatment (as long as it won't break the bank and cause more stress).
- Play on the playground with your kids (or swing by yourself).
- Watch a movie.

ESCAPE FROM EXHAUSTION

Amy Lynn Andrews, mom of four, blogger at BloggingWithAmy .com and my friend whom I talked about in chapter 2, experienced her own season of burnout and exhaustion. I asked her to share how she was able to pull herself through that trying time and how she is preventing future breakdowns.

By the end of the summer of 2012, I was struggling. I had been working full-time for a year, but I felt like I was spinning my wheels. My progress didn't seem to be in line with my output, and my choices didn't seem to be getting me closer to my goals.

A few things contributed to my overall stress level. One was lack of sleep. I have trouble sleeping, so a deliberate routine is imperative. Because I was discouraged with the amount of things not getting done, I was staying up much later than I should have. I thought this way, I'd be able to make up for the things that didn't get done during the day. Of course, this only got me caught up in a vicious cycle.

Two, I lacked a plan. Over the last few years, I've learned I am great at coming up with ideas, but not so great at implementing them. My to-do list was filled with worthwhile tasks, but I lacked a concrete plan to get them done. Without a plan, I was filling my time with distractions (social media, munching, surfing the web, reading, etc.), clearly contributing to the spinning-my-wheels feeling.

Three, I'm a perfectionist. I'm the type of person who knows exactly what I want. I've been known to spend obscene amounts of time on trivial details. One of my main sticking points occurs when one of my to-do items is completed well enough, but not perfectly. I have a hard time considering it done and moving on. Instead, I leave it and tell myself I'll refine it later. Of course, it often sits there unfinished indefinitely.

My wake-up call began when I was lamenting to my husband about my lack of motivation one morning. He made a very simple statement that really hit me. He gently said, "Are you actually doing something or just moving furniture around?" Of course he was speaking metaphorically, but for some reason, it made me think of my situation in a new way.

I have since learned to reach out for help. I hired an assistant who relieves me of those tasks that have been sitting on my to-do list for a long time. I also realized I'm not nearly as perfectionistic when someone else is handling it. I buttoned up my bedtime routine, but I relaxed my wake-up routine. It may sound counterintuitive, but I had convinced myself that I needed to wake up very early in order to be productive. This might be true if I wasn't so completely exhausted by the time 5 a.m. rolled around because I had only slept a few hours. Now, if I go to bed at a decent hour but don't sleep well, I give myself permission to move a bit slower in the mornings knowing I'll last longer throughout the day. I also finally sat down and wrote out the ideas and plans I had in my head. Getting them on paper allowed me to see where there were holes.

TREAT YOURSELF WITH GRACE AND KINDNESS

One thing I've noticed is that, outside of comparing ourselves to others, women are notorious for beating ourselves up for not doing or being everything we want to do or be. For some women, this feeling can be paralyzing.

Let me assure you of a few things. You are never going to be exactly where you want to be. There will always be another project, another chore, another task, or another idea to get started. And as soon as you complete one thing, there's another one (or five) that needs to get done.

So don't beat yourself up that you're not as far as you'd like to be. Instead, be kind to yourself and give yourself grace. Focus on the positive, like the progress you have made and are making. Rather than being disappointed that you have six outstanding items left on your to-do list and it's already ten thirty at night, be encouraged that you accomplished three of the things you set out to do today.

When you have a day when it seems like nothing gets done and you're just going around and around in circles, remind yourself that tomorrow is a new day. And slow down!

If you incorporate some of these tips into your life, you know what will happen? You'll ultimately see an increase in your energy stores. You'll feel better. You'll feel more alive. You might even find a spring in your step that you never thought you had. You'll have more passion for life, and this will allow you to devote time and energy to what matters most—versus spending most of your days just trying to make it through the day.

GET PRACTICAL

Think of your life as a pie. Section the slices into the areas you focus on every day. For instance, work, family, friendships, spiritual matters, fun, health. Now think about how much of your time and energy is being poured into each area. Ask yourself the following questions:

- Am I living a balanced life?
- Am I spending time on my priorities?
- Am I spending time on things that matter most?
- What needs less attention? More attention?
- What changes do I need to make?

After reflecting on these questions, decide what you need to do to better care for yourself. Then do it!

10 ■ ■■ ■■■■■ ■■ ■■■■ ■■■ ■■■■ ■

Kick-Start Your Success

> The difference between who you are and
> who you want to be is what you do.
> —BILL PHILLIPS

As I've been writing this book, I've been knitting scarves for my daughters. I'm not an experienced knitter by any stretch of the imagination, but I love challenging myself to learn new things and becoming more proficient in handwork. Plus, I love to multitask. Knitting is a great way to use those moments while I'm chatting with a friend or we're watching a movie as a family to also do something with my hands.

Ever since I started, my daughter, Kaitlynn has been watching me knit and begging me to teach her. So the other day I pulled out some yarn and needles and we had a knitting lesson. She was eager to learn—so eager, in fact, that she wanted to skip right through the basics and try to make hand warmers (I love that girl's ambition!).

As I was showing Kaitlynn how to cast on and do the knit stitch, she was getting impatient at how tedious the process was. She quickly flipped ahead to a more difficult pattern in the instruction book and asked if we could please make that. My advice to her had to do with the many life lessons I've learned the hard way: "You have to do the little things before you can do the big things."

This book is made up of suggestions of little things that make up the big picture.

- Remember you are not Superwoman, and release yourself from the pressure to do everything.
- Learn to prioritize what's most important and focus on the best stuff.
- Set goals and take the right steps to accomplish them.
- Understand the art and importance of discipline to streamline your life and get things done.
- Get ahold of your finances for the right reasons, and manage your money purposefully.
- Take care of your home and day-to-day responsibilities in a simple way so you have time to do things that matter most (like loving on your loved ones).
- Learn how to move forward when distractions, life-changing events, and setbacks occur on your journey of living on purpose.
- Look beyond yourself and make a difference in the needs of those around you and around the world.
- Practice self-care to be a better woman overall.

It might seem that those little goals—like getting to bed on time, exercising consistently, saying no more often, and cutting out physical and calendar clutter—aren't going to make that big of an impact. I know the feeling. We're all impatient. We want to run ahead and enjoy that great success, land that amazing job, or knit that incredible pattern. Now.

But it's rare that you can jump ahead in life and do difficult things (and reap the rewards) if you haven't first started and mastered the simple things. Yes, it involves doing a lot of the same stuff over and over again. It can be time-consuming and tedious. And it takes time to see progress. But those little things are often the start of very big things.

Just like knitting a beautiful scarf requires doing one stitch at a time, so in your life, you need to do the little things over and over again. Over time, those little things all add together to make a big difference in your life—like the beautiful scarf I finished recently.

I'm delighted you have stayed the course with me on this journey. You may already be experiencing some big changes in your life. Or you might have tabled some of my suggestions and are now finally ready to implement them into your life.

If you have not yet begun to dive in to some of the practices you've learned in this book, I encourage you to take the next step and implement the following seven habits that I am confident will change your life. Commit to doing one every week. The habits will build on themselves, and by the end of two months, you'll be in a much better place than you are now.

If adding a new habit every week for seven weeks seems overwhelming, just pick one to focus on for the next month. Don't get hung up if it takes you longer than a week to work on a habit. Remember: moving in the right direction, even at a snail's pace, is still moving forward!

SEVEN HABITS THAT WILL CHANGE YOUR LIFE

1. **Start taking care of yourself.** If you don't put a priority on your health and mental sanity, you will pay for it now and later. Not only will you be constantly overworked, exhausted, and stressed, but you'll also suffer from the physical and emotional fallout that comes from not making yourself a priority.

2. **Go to bed early and get a good night's rest.** Most Americans are severely sleep deprived. It's no wonder they don't have passion and purpose for life; they can barely keep their eyes open and their heads from nodding off! Refueling your sleep tank is important to being efficient during the day.

3. **Make the most of your mornings.** Getting your day off to a great start is one of the best ways to kick-start your productivity. Wake up a little earlier, and spend time building your faith by reading the Bible and praying. Start tackling a few items on your to-do list. Make a goal list for the week. Go for a walk around your neighborhood.

4. **Set five small goals.** Without goals, all your good intentions amount to nothing. You need concrete, realistic goals if you want to make traction in the right direction.

5. **Break down your goals into bite-size pieces.** Sometimes a big goal can seem overwhelming. Break down your big goals into monthly, then weekly chunks—things you can accomplish in fifteen to thirty minutes at a time. You'll instantly transform your goals from daunting to doable.

6. **Find an accountability partner.** You can't live life on purpose on your own. Find a friend or two who are willing to

keep you on task. Set up regular check-ins, whether online, in person, or over the phone. Share ideas on how to practically engage in an accountability relationship.

7. **Replace the TV or Internet surfing with productivity.** Feel like you don't have enough time? Well, you're not alone. Most Americans feel like they are incredibly strapped for time. But the average American also watches four hours of television per day. If we all invested even half of that time into improving ourselves, working toward our goals, working out, getting more sleep, and so on, think about how much better we'd feel and how much more fulfilled we'd be in life!

SAY HELLO TO A LIFE THAT MATTERS

When I was eleven years old, I committed my life to Christ. From that day forward, I've constantly lived with the realization that I only have one shot at life—and that my time on earth is finite.

I didn't have any amazing gifts or talents. I was pretty much just an average girl who got average grades and lived an average American life. But I wanted something more. I didn't want to be content with average.

So I started reading voraciously. I set my alarm to get up early. I set goals and worked toward them. I began investing every day thinking of what would matter most at the end of my life. All of those little things added up to a life changed.

At the time, it didn't seem like it was making a big impact. But now, twenty years later, those daily choices have added up to shape me into where I am today: blogging, writing, speaking, and, most of all, loving my life! Yes, there are hard things. Yes, I make many mistakes. But I get up every day excited about what lies before me. Eager to meet the day and the challenges. Anxious to make a little more traction each day toward bigger goals I have for the future.

No matter your age, your financial situation, your education, or your upbringing, you can live an exceptional life. You can say goodbye to survival mode and hello to a life that matters. A life that makes a difference. A life on purpose!

Appendix ▮▮▮▮▮▮▮▮▮▮▮▮▮▮▮▮▮▮▮▮▮

My Goals This Week

DATE _____

| MARRIAGE | | TO REMEMBER |

CHILDREN

HOME MANAGEMENT

PERSONAL

BLOGGING

MINISTRY

> "Without **goals**, and **plans** to reach them, you are like a **ship** that has set sail with no **destination**.
>
> FITZHUGH DODSON

My Goals

Priority 1
Focus Areas

Priority 2
Focus Areas

Priority 3
Focus Areas

Priority 4
Focus Areas

Priority 5
Focus Areas

Priority 6
Focus Areas

My Daily Docket

M Tu W Th F Sa Su

todo

☐ **bible**reading

☐ **weekly**chores

BEFORE BREAKFAST
☐ Shower & Dress
☐ Make Bed
☐ Clean Room & Bathroom
☐ Start Load of Laundry

AFTER BREAKFAST
☐ Clean Up Breakfast Dishes
☐ Unload & Load Dishwasher
☐ Wipe Kitchen Countertops
☐ Thaw Anything Needed for Dinner
☐ 5-Minute Pickup
☐ Switch Load of Laundry

AFTER LUNCH
☐ Clean Up Lunch Dishes
☐ Load Dishwasher
☐ Sweep Kitchen Floor
☐ 5-Minute Pickup
☐ Clean Front Door/Back Door Glass

BEFORE DINNER
☐ Dinner Prep
☐ Fold Load of Laundry & Put Away
☐ 5-Minute Pickup

AFTER DINNER
☐ Clean Up Dinner Dishes
☐ Load Dishwasher & Run

☐ **exercise**

☐☐☐☐☐☐☐☐☐☐

tobuy

ourdinner

toblog

extraprojects/ministry

*Find a customizable Daily Docket on MoneySavingMom.com.

Recommended Resources

LIVING WITH PURPOSE

Cordeiro, Wayne. *Leading on Empty: Refilling Your Tank and Renewing Your Passion.* Ada, MI: Bethany House, 2010.

Swenson, Dr. Richard. *A Minute of Margin: Restoring Balance to Busy Lives.* Colorado Springs, CO: NavPress, 2003.

Swenson, Dr. Richard. *Margin: Restoring Emotional, Physical, Financial, and Time Reserves to Overloaded Lives.* Colorado Springs, CO: NavPress, 2004.

TIME MANAGEMENT

Andrews, Amy Lynn. *Tell Your Time: How to Manage Your Schedule So You Can Live Free.* Amazon Digital Services, 2011.

Duhigg, Charles. *The Power of Habit: Why We Do What We Do in Life and Business.* New York, NY: Random House, 2012.

Tracy, Brian. *Eat That Frog! 21 Great Ways to Stop Procrastinating and Get More Done in Less Time.* 2nd ed. San Francisco, CA: Berrett-Koehler Publishers, 2007.

Vanderkam, Laura. *168 Hours: You Have More Time Than You Think.* New York, NY: Portfolio, 2010.

Vanderkam, Laura. *What the Most Successful People Do Before Breakfast: A Short Guide to Making Over Your Mornings—and Life.* New York, NY: Penguin, 2012.

FINANCIAL MANAGEMENT

Dacyczyn, Amy. *The Complete Tightwad Gazette*. New York, NY: Villard, 1998.

Economides, Steve and Annette Economides. *America's Cheapest Family Gets You Right on the Money: Your Guide to Living Better, Spending Less, and Cashing in on Your Dreams*. New York, NY: Three Rivers Press, 2007.

McCoy, Jonni. *Miserly Moms: Living Well on Less in a Tough Economy*. Colorado Springs, CO: Bethany, 2009.

Ramsey, Dave. *Total Money Makeover: A Proven Plan for Financial Fitness*. Nashville, TN: Thomas Nelson, 2009.

HOME MANAGEMENT

Allen, David. *Getting Things Done: The Art of Stress-Free Productivity*. New York, NY: Penguin, 2002.

Bowen, Lynn. *Queen of the Castle: 52 Weeks of Encouragement for the Uninspired, Domestically Challenged, or Just Plain Tired*. Nashville, TN: Thomas Nelson, 2006.

Fisher, Jessica. *Not Your Mother's Make Ahead and Freeze Cookbook*. Boston, MA: Harvard Common Press, 2012.

Ostyn, Mary. *A Sane Woman's Guide to Raising a Large Family*. Layton, UT: Gibbs Smith, 2009.

Oxenreider, Tsh. *Organized Simplicity: The Clutter-Free Approach to Intentional Living*. Cincinnati, OH: Betterway Home, 2010.

Twigg, Nancy. *From Clutter to Clarity: Simplifying Life from the Inside Out*. Cincinnati, OH: Standard, 2007.

FITNESS AND NUTRITION

Parham, Phil and Amy. *The 90-Day Fitness Challenge: A Proven Program for Better Health and Lasting Weight Loss*. Eugene, OR: Harvest House, 2010.

PRACTICAL HELP

DeMoss, Nancy Leigh. *Choosing Gratitude: Your Journey to Joy.* Chicago, IL: Moody, 2011.

Dillow, Linda. *Calm My Anxious Heart: A Woman's Guide to Finding Contentment.* Colorado Springs, CO: NavPress, 2007.

Dillow, Linda. *Satisfy My Thirsty Soul: For I Am Desperate for Your Presence.* Colorado Springs, CO: NavPress, 2007.

Gerth, Holley. *You're Already Amazing: Embracing Who You Are, Becoming All God Created You to Be.* Ada, MI: Revell, 2012.

Jankovic, Rachael. *Loving the Little Years: Motherhood in the Trenches.* Stafford, VA: Canon, 2010.

Stephens, Steve and Alice Gray. *The Worn Out Woman: When Life Is Full and Your Spirit Is Empty.* Sisters, OR: Multnomah, 2004.

Swope, Renee. *A Confident Heart: How to Stop Doubting Yourself and Live in the Security of God's Promises.* Ada, MI: Revell, 2011.

Westerfield, Kelly. *Trend Breakers: Discovering and Choosing True Friendship in a Lonely World.* Amazon Digital Services, 2012.

ENJOYMENT

Chapman, Mary Beth. *Choosing to SEE: A Journey of Struggle and Hope.* Ada, MI: Revell, 2011.

Diebler Rose, Darlene. *Evidence Not Seen: A Woman's Miraculous Faith in the Jungles of World War II.* New York, NY: HarperOne, 2003.

Smith, Angie. *I Will Carry You: The Sacred Dance of Grief and Joy.* Nashville, TN: B&H Publishing Group, 2010.

Ten Boom, Corrie. *The Hiding Place: The Triumphant Story of Corrie Ten Boom.* New York, NY: Random House, 1984.

Notes ▊▊▊▊▊▊▊▊▊▊▊▊▊▊▊▊▊▊▊▊▊▊▊

Chapter 1: Stop Trying to Do It All

1. Dr. Richard Swenson, *Margin: Restoring Emotional, Physical, Financial, and Time Reserves to Overloaded Lives* (Colorado Springs, CO: NavPress, 2004), 69.

Chapter 2: Say Yes to the Best

1. Laura Vanderkam, *168 Hours: You Have More Time Than You Think* (New York, NY: Portfolio, 2010), chapter 2.
2. Institute of Medicine, *Sleep Disorders and Sleep Deprivation: An Unmet Public Health Problem* (Washington, DC: The National Academies Press, 2006).
3. Ibid.

Chapter 4: Discipline Is Not a Bad Word

1. LeechBlock is a productivity tool available on the Firefox web browser, designed to block time-wasting sites during times you specify. For more information about LeechBlock or to download this free app, go to https://addons.mozilla.org/en-us/firefox/addon /leechblock/.
2. Brian Tracy, *Eat That Frog! 21 Great Ways to Stop Procrastinating and Get More Done in Less Time* , 2nd ed. (San Francisco, CA: Berrett-Koehler Publishers, 2007).
3. Charles Duhigg, *The Power of Habit: Why We Do What We Do in Life and Business* (New York, NY: Random House, 2012).
4. Charles Duhigg, "The Right Habits," *LifeHacker* (blog), April 2, 2012, http://lifehacker.com/5896846/the-right-habits.

Chapter 5: Be Intentional with Your Bank Account

1. Dave Ramsey, *The Total Money Makeover: A Proven Plan for Financial Fitness* (Nashville, TN: Thomas Nelson, 2009).
2. To learn more about Financial Peace University and find a class near you, go to http://www.daveramsey.com/fpu.

Chapter 8: Yes, You Can Make a Difference

1. To learn more about Compassion International and find out how you can donate to the Child Survival Program, go to http://www.compassion.com/child-survival-program.htm.

Chapter 9: Sometimes It *Is* About You

1. Rachael Jankovic, *Loving the Little Years: Motherhood in the Trenches* (Stafford, VA: Canon, 2010), 14.
2. Ann Voskamp, "How Hurting Women Can Help Each Other Heal," A Holy Experience (blog), April 26, 2011, http://www.aholyexperience.com/2011/04/how-hurting-women-can-help-each-other-heal/.
3. Arabah Joy, *Energy Explosion: A 7-Day Guide to Jumpstart Your Energy* (Amazon Digital Services, 2012).
4. Collette Bouchez, "How Much Exercise Do You Really Need?" WebMD, accessed June 25, 2013, http://www.webmd.com/fitness-exercise/features/getting-enough-exercise.

Acknowledgments

While this book has my name on the cover, it wouldn't have happened without an army of people:

My agent, Esther: Thank you for catching a vision from the start and making it a reality. I'm grateful for you!

My ghost-editor, AJ: This book is at least twenty times better because of you!

My initial manuscript reviewers (Alanna, Anne, Ashley, Carrie, Catherine, Ellen, and Zan): Thank you for your honest critiques; they made the manuscript much stronger.

My editor, Bryan N.: You went well beyond the call of duty. (I'm confident most editors don't wake up at 3 a.m. to give their best to a project!)

My team at Thomas Nelson: I cannot sing your praises enough. You've far exceeded my expectations!

My amazing managers, Brian S. & Joy G.: Thank you for being my burden-bearers and wise counselors, and for challenging me to continually stretch myself. I owe much to you.

My team (Erika, Liz, Joy M., Jeff, Lisa, Gretchen, Nathaniel, Amy, Brigette, and Andrea): Thank you for investing your time and talents into MoneySavingMom.com. I couldn't have written this book without you all!

My treasured friends (Angie D., Jerica, Susanna, Katherine, Angie S., Kathi, Michele, Angie R., Renee, Ruth, Jenae, Stacie):

Thank you for being people who will drop everything to pray for me or listen to me. I love you dearly.

My blog readers: What started out as a little writing outlet for me has become a wonderful community of people I can't imagine living life without. Thank you for showing up every day and blessing me with your encouraging comments. You mean the world to me.

My siblings, extended family, and in-laws: Thank you for how you enrich my life, keep me grounded, and make me laugh. Oh, the memories we have made and continue to make!

My mom and dad: You are the most giving, selfless people I've ever met. Thank you for challenging me not be content with the status quo but to instead live a life sold-out for Christ. I love you!

My precious children, Kathrynne, Kaitlynn, and Silas: Becoming your mom is one of the best things that has ever happened to me. I'm so proud of you and excited about what God has in store for your futures! I love you more with each passing day.

My incredible husband, Jesse: You are my biggest cheerleader, my greatest confidante, and my best friend. Thank you for dreaming big dreams with me, believing Ephesians 3:20 with me, loving me no matter what, and shooting it straight—even when I don't always want to hear your wise counsel! I love you more than words can say and would marry you all over again.

My Heavenly Father: Without You, I would have no life, breath, or purpose. You are my everything. It is my heart's desire to live a life poured out for You and that someday I may hear the words, "Well done, good and faithful servant." Nothing else matters.